'Botvinick's lively introduction [provides] insight into the play's possib[le] textual and performative histo[ry...] tive commentary, which enables the reader to visualize and work through the practical demands of the play in performance.' – Peter Kirwan, *University of Nottingham, UK*

'This book offers fascinating insights into the dramatist's satire of greed, materialism and bestiality, while usefully situating the play in both early modern and contemporary theatrical contexts. Both first-time students of Jonson and teachers will find this handbook extremely useful.' – Shehzana Mamujee, *Newcastle University, UK*

One of the blackest comedies ever written, Ben Jonson's *Volpone* is the masterpiece of a playwright all too frequently dismissed for being unnecessarily dark and academic. Merciless in its depiction of avarice, this rich and masterful play provokes both laughter and indignation in its audiences.

This Handbook:

- Provides in-depth analysis of the play, scene by scene and line by line
- Examines the multitude of interpretations of *Volpone* throughout history, including both on stage and on screen
- Explores the critical discourse surrounding the play and summarizes the social and literary forces that shaped Jonson's work.

Marshall Botvinick is Lecturer in the Department of Theatre at the University of North Carolina Wilmington, USA. He is also a professional dramaturg who has worked with the American Repertory Theater, PlayMakers Repertory Company, and Burning Coal Theatre Company.

The Shakespeare Handbooks are student-friendly introductory guides which offer a new approach to understanding the plays of Shakespeare and his contemporaries in performance. The commentary at the heart of each volume explores the play's theatrical potential, providing an experience as close as possible to seeing it in the theatre. Ideal for students and teachers of Literature and Theatre, as well as actors and directors, the overall aim is to help a reader reach an independent and well-informed view of each play by imagining how it might be rehearsed or performed on stage.

THE SHAKESPEARE HANDBOOKS

Series Editors: Paul Edmondson and Kevin Ewert
(Founding Series Editor: John Russell Brown)

PUBLISHED

David Carnegie	*Julius Caesar*
Paul Edmondson	*Twelfth Night*
Bridget Escolme	*Antony and Cleopatra*
Kevin Ewert	*Henry V*
Alison Findlay	*Much Ado About Nothing*
Trevor R. Griffiths	*The Tempest*
Stuart Hampton-Reeves	*Measure for Measure*
Stuart Hampton-Reeves	*Othello*
Margaret Jane Kidnie	*The Taming of the Shrew*
Ros King	*The Winter's Tale*
James N. Loehlin	*Henry IV: Parts I and II*
Jeremy Lopez	*Richard II*
Christopher McCullough	*The Merchant of Venice*
Paul Prescott	*Richard III*
Edward L. Rocklin	*Romeo and Juliet*
John Russell Brown	*Hamlet*
John Russell Brown	*King Lear*
John Russell Brown	*Macbeth*
Lesley Wade Soule	*As You Like It*
Martin White	*A Midsummer Night's Dream*

SHAKESPEARE'S CONTEMPORARIES

Marshall Botvinick	Jonson: *Volpone*
David Carnegie	Webster: *The Duchess of Malfi*
Jay O'Berski	Middleton and Rowley: *The Changeling*
Stephen Purcell	Webster: *The White Devil*
Martin White	Ford: *'Tis Pity She's a Whore*

Other titles are currently in preparation.

The Shakespeare Handbooks
Shakespeare's Contemporaries

Ben Jonson
Volpone

Marshall Botvinick

© Marshall Botvinick 2015

All rights reserved. No reproduction, copy or transmission of this publication may be made without written permission.

No portion of this publication may be reproduced, copied or transmitted save with written permission or in accordance with the provisions of the Copyright, Designs and Patents Act 1988, or under the terms of any licence permitting limited copying issued by the Copyright Licensing Agency, Saffron House, 6–10 Kirby Street, London EC1N 8TS.

Any person who does any unauthorized act in relation to this publication may be liable to criminal prosecution and civil claims for damages.

The author has asserted his right to be identified as the author of this work in accordance with the Copyright, Designs and Patents Act 1988.

First published 2015 by
PALGRAVE

Palgrave in the UK is an imprint of Macmillan Publishers Limited, registered in England, company number 7898, of 4 Crinan Street, London, N1 9XW.

Palgrave Macmillan in the US is a division of St Martin's Press LLC, 175 Fifth Avenue, New York, NY 10010.

Palgrave Macmillan is a global imprint of the above companies and is represented throughout the world.

Palgrave® and Macmillan® are registered trademarks in the United States, the United Kingdom, Europe and other countries.

ISBN: 978–1–137–37981–8 hardback
ISBN: 978–1–137–37980–1 paperback

This book is printed on paper suitable for recycling and made from fully managed and sustained forest sources. Logging, pulping and manufacturing processes are expected to conform to the environmental regulations of the country of origin.

A catalogue record for this book is available from the British Library.

A catalog record for this book is available from the Library of Congress.

Printed in China

For my mom, who taught me all I know about the English language and 98% of what she knows

Contents

Series Editors' Preface		viii
Preface		ix
1	The Text and Early Performances	1
2	Cultural Contexts and Sources	7
3	Commentary	19
4	Key Productions and Performances	84
5	The Play on Screen	102
6	Critical Assessments	111
Further Reading		127
Index		133

Series Editors' Preface

The Shakespeare Handbooks provide an innovative way of studying the plays of Shakespeare and his contemporaries in performance. The commentaries, which are their core feature, enable a reader to envisage the words of a text unfurling in performance, involving actions and meanings not readily perceived except in rehearsal or performance. The aim is to present the plays in the environment for which they were written and to offer an experience as close as possible to an audience's progressive experience of a production.

While each book has the same range of contents, their authors have been encouraged to shape them according to their own critical and scholarly understanding and their first-hand experience of theater practice. The various chapters are designed to complement the commentaries: the cultural context of each play is presented together with quotations from original sources; the authority of its text or texts is considered with what is known of the earliest performances; key performances and productions of its subsequent stage history are both described and compared; an account is given of influential criticism of the play and the more significant is quoted extensively. The aim in all this has been to help readers to develop their own informed and imaginative view of a play in ways that supplement the provision of standard editions and are more user friendly than detailed stage histories or collections of criticism from diverse sources.

We would like to acknowledge a special debt of gratitude to the founder of the Shakespeare Handbooks Series, John Russell Brown, whose energy for life, literature and theater we continue to find truly inspiring.

Paul Edmondson and Kevin Ewert

Preface

So much has been written about Ben Jonson and his masterful comedy *Volpone* that it can be daunting to say something original and valuable, but the text is so rich with meaning and possibility that after nearly two years of research and writing I cannot help but feel that so much has still been left unsaid. What follows here is my best attempt to give new and returning readers of this 400-year-old play a sense of the tremendous power that this work possesses on the page and, more importantly, on the stage.

Thanks to: Jay O'Berski for thinking of me when this opportunity first arose, my wife for silently enduring the ever-growing stack of books about Ben Jonson and Jacobean performance that overran our guest bedroom like a plague of scholastic kudzu, directors Michael Kahn and Greg Hersov for being generous enough to speak with me about their productions of *Volpone*, and my many academic mentors for not letting me settle for mediocre work.

Mostly, though, I am indebted to Kevin Ewert for not only trusting me to write this book but also for encouraging and challenging me throughout this long but rewarding endeavor. This book would not have been possible without his guidance and feedback.

M.A.B.

1 The Text and Early Performances

The text

In his 1973 essay 'Jonson and the Loathèd Stage', Jonas Barish persuasively argues that both Jonson's life and work are pregnant with an antitheatrical prejudice. Visible in every aspect of Jonson's writing, Barish claims, are a deep-seated distrust of the theatrical experience and an undeniable preference for the printed word. In the decades following Barish's essay, many scholars have sought to temper this perception of Jonson as an enemy of the stage; however, even those scholars who defend Jonson as a man of the theater still concede that he, alone among renowned Elizabethan and Jacobean playwrights, took an active role in the preparing and printing of dramatic texts for publication. Why was Jonson unique in this regard? What did he have to gain from the publication of his plays? And what were the consequences of Jonson's involvement in the preparing of his dramatic texts for print?

Because Jonson inserted himself so heavily into the publication process, his scripts reflect authorial intent in a way that most scripts from this era do not. In contrast to Shakespeare, whose 1623 Folio was prepared seven years after his death, Jonson published his Folio, the first of its kind by an English dramatist, 21 years before his death. *Volpone*, written in 1606, is one of nine plays included in the 1616 Folio prepared by Jonson. In addition to the version published in the 1616 Folio, there is the 1607 Quarto of *Volpone*. (There are also two posthumously published folios, one in 1640 and one in 1692, but these texts are notoriously unreliable and hold no textual authority.) Unlike many of Shakespeare's plays, which often exhibit numerous discrepancies between Q and F, *Volpone* contains only small variations from Q to F; and the variations that do exist are limited almost exclusively to punctuation (more punctuation in F than Q), minor stage directions (less incidental stage directions in Q than F) and isolated word choices.

Jonson's passionate feelings about the dissemination of his plays in print are strange since publication was an economic liability for Jacobean playwrights. Without copyright laws to protect their work, dramatists who published their writing were inviting rival theater companies to take their popular plays and perform them free of charge. This risk, however, did not deter Jonson. In fact, he favored the printed word because it offered him two things that public performances could not: permanence and the chance to have a controlled conversation with a well-schooled reader. Throughout his career Jonson fought to preserve his writing for posterity, but a performance by its very nature is ephemeral. For a man so concerned with the destiny of his corpus, it must have been inconceivable to write solely for such a fleeting medium. Furthermore, the printed word allowed Jonson to control the reception and interpretation of his work. In the theater, which is a collaborative art, it would have been impossible for him to exert such control, for the conveyance of meaning passes through multiple mediators before it reaches its intended destination: actors interpret and, in Jacobean times, interpolate text; and rowdy audience members comment on the production, thereby shaping the perceptions of others in the crowd. In publication, however, Jonson could find a direct line to his target audience and manipulate their reactions from the first word to the last.

Quite frequently Jonson prefaces his texts with elaborate dedications and lengthy statements that are designed to embed a certain set of ideas in the minds of his readers before they begin the play, and *Volpone* arguably represents the best example of this tactic. (The 1607 Quarto contains 18 pages of prefatory writing between the title page and the beginning of the play. Even Jonson jokes about the size of his introduction, noting on the dedication page that 'there follows an Epistle, if you dare venture on the length'.) Jonson utilizes the Epistle to weigh in on the moral character of his person and writing as well as to comment on the decidedly uncomic ending of his comedy. In both matters Jonson's Epistle, like program notes in modern productions, is attempting to predetermine the way his readers approach the text. In doing so, it seizes control of the play's meaning and challenges anyone to see the text in a different light than the author intended.

Jonson had a vested interest in proving to his readership that his comedy about criminals, con men, freaks and sexual deviants contained nothing controversial or immoral. As a Catholic convert living in a Protestant country, Jonson was looked upon with suspicion by the authorities. Furthermore, he had a long history with the law, including a 1598 murder conviction for which he remarkably escaped the death penalty by pleading 'Benefit of Clergy'. Even his previous play, *Eastward Ho*, resulted in a trip to prison and a threat of 'ear cropping' and 'nose slitting' because it offended James I. Consequently, Jonson, who wrote *Volpone* shortly after his release from prison, could not afford to have his next play misconstrued or interpreted in an unflattering manner. It is for these reasons that Jonson includes the following warnings and disclaimers in his Epistle:

> I can – and from a most clear conscience – affirm that I have ever trembled to think toward the least profaneness, have loathed the use of such foul and unwashed bawdry as is now made the food of the scene. (ll. 40–3)

And:

> There are that profess to have a key for the deciphering of everything; but let wise and noble persons take heed how they be too credulous, or give leave to these invading interpreters to be overfamiliar with their fames, who cunningly, and often, utter their own virulent malice under other men's simplest meanings. (ll. 60–4)

By labeling critics of *Volpone* 'invading interpreters', Jonson casts himself as an innocent victim of slander and libel, and he instills doubt in any reader who suspects the play might contain seditious or immoral content. To advance his argument, Jonson claims that the task of a good poet – and the self-adoring Jonson certainly fancied himself that and more – is to 'inform men in the best reason of living' (ll. 99–100). Seen in this light, *Volpone* functions as a morality tale that decries vice and cautions against the excess of greed. Although this is certainly not the most interesting reading of the play, it is the one that Jonson needed in 1607 to ensure his safety.

As for the play's ending, Jonson is caught between two neoclassical dictums: the purity of genres and the demand that evil be punished. If the titular character does not receive his comeuppance, then sin goes unpunished; however, if he does suffer the negative consequences of his actions (as happens in the play), then the work ceases to be a comedy in the traditional sense. A devoted neoclassicist, Jonson uses the Epistle to justify the dark – some would say tragic – conclusion of his comedy. Jonson asks the 'charitable critic' (l. 102) to trust in the intentionality of his ending, and he claims:

> My special aim being to put the snaffle in their mouths that cry out we never punish vice ... it being the office of a comic poet to imitate justice and instruct to life. (ll. 105–12)

Thus, the Epistle serves as the venue in which Jonson redefines the function of comedy and wards off the neoclassical critics who would accuse him of violating a sacrosanct law of the genre. It also braces readers for *Volpone*'s nontraditional ending, thereby making them less likely to suffer the outrage that typically accompanies violated expectations.

In short, what is interesting about the printing and distribution of *Volpone* is not the textual history, which is remarkably straightforward for the early 17th century, but the way in which the extratextual material included in the initial publication has shaped the debate and conversation surrounding *Volpone* for more than four centuries.

Early performances

Written in a feverishly quick five weeks in the winter of 1606, *Volpone* was first performed by the King's Men in either February or March of 1606. The 1616 Folio identifies six actors (Richard Burbage, John Heminges, Henry Condell, John Lowin, William Sly and Alexander Cooke) as the 'principal comedians' in the original production. Although the Folio does not specify which actor played which role, it is universally assumed that Richard Burbage, the greatest actor of his era, played Volpone. By all available accounts, the play was a great success. After its London premiere, it received the rare honor of being presented at both Oxford and Cambridge, an honor that

Jonson acknowledges in his dedication to 'the two famous universities, for their love and acceptance' (Dedication, ll. 2–3). There are also records of successful revivals in 1624, 1630 and 1638. The triumph of *Volpone* could not have come at a more favorable time for Jonson, whose previous two plays – *Sejanus* and *Eastward Ho* – resulted in a hissing audience and jail time respectively.

Throughout his career Jonson alternated between premiering his work at large public playhouses, which featured adult actors, and small private playhouses, which featured boys' companies. Audience members at public playhouses were rambunctious and eager for entertainment that could rival the activities at the bear-baiting pits and brothels located near the theaters. Attendees of the private theaters, on the other hand, tended to be more erudite and typically hailed from the upper crust of English society. Jonson presumably knew that *Volpone* would first be presented at the Globe, one of London's most important public theaters; therefore, it is logical to assume that he tailored his writing to the tastes of the public theatergoer and the talents of the professional actor. *Volpone* is a highly kinetic work that relies on broad physical comedy and rapid activity. In addition, *Volpone* is less scholarly than many of Jonson's plays that were presented in private playhouses; for example, *Epicene*, written immediately after *Volpone* and presented by a children's company at the noted private playhouse Whitefriars, includes a climactic scene that is nearly incomprehensible to any audience member not proficient in Latin. Comparatively, *Volpone* contains relatively few Latin phrases. The opportunity to write for a troupe of professional adult actors, as opposed to children with smaller skillsets, also seems to have affected the composition of *Volpone*. Unlike members of the boys' companies, the veteran performers in the King's Men were ready and able to handle numerous lengthy speeches as well as the complicated physical and vocal adjustments associated with the play's heavy reliance on disguise. In short, the profound effect of the original performance conditions on the text cannot be overlooked.

Even after Jonson's death in 1637, *Volpone* remained a popular staple of the English theater until the late 18th century. When theaters reopened in 1660, *Volpone* was quickly and successfully revived at court. In a 1665 entry, the famous English diarist Samuel Pepys deemed *Volpone* to be 'a most excellent play; the best I think I ever saw'. After a brief absence in the late 17th century, *Volpone* returned to the English stage with even more regularity in the beginning of the 18th century, receiving approximately one or two performances a year for the first quarter of the century. It was also during this period that the first published review of *Volpone* appeared, with critic Richard Steele praising Jonson for his remarkably specific and varied characters. Despite minor complaints about superfluous characters and an implausible final act, *Volpone* remained a respected piece of drama through most of the 18th century; however, signs of its demise became evident when condensed versions of the play were mounted in 1771 and 1783. As theater historian Robert Noyes points out, 'Two hours and a half was the normal time required for tragedies, most comedies requiring two hours or less. Of Jonson's plays, *Volpone* demanded the longest playing-time, and the managers were becoming conscious that revision was advisable' (p. 89). Not even a more streamlined text, however, could insulate *Volpone* from the changing tastes of the English public. In 1785 it was quietly revived one last time before disappearing from the stage for 136 years before the Phoenix Society revived it in 1921. Reasons for *Volpone*'s disappearance from the stage are manifold. They include the play's aforementioned length, its 'excessive Latinity' (an ironic charge when one thinks of other plays by Jonson), its strict adherence to neoclassical principles (principles scorned and discarded by the Romantics of the late 18th and early 19th century) and its unapologetic depiction of vice and sexual depravity (something abhorrent to the upright Victorians of the late 19th century). Fortunately, these limiting preferences were abandoned in the early 20th century, and *Volpone* has once again gained the appreciation it so clearly deserves.

2 Cultural Contexts and Sources

Economic context

The Age of Jonson was a transitional time for England. The country still cleaved to certain relics of the medieval economy, but it was also beginning to adopt many aspects of the modern capitalist system. Some prominent features of the medieval economy were the active role played by guilds, the general absence of social or financial mobility and the existence of a localized market that ensured most transactions took place within the confines of a close-knit community. Even though these vestiges of the medieval economy could still be observed during the Elizabethan-Jacobean era, they were undeniably on the decline. Replacing them were a slew of capitalist innovations that were timed perfectly to the circumstances of the late 16th and early 17th century. Between 1550 and 1600 the population of London ballooned from approximately 50,000 to 200,000 people. This sizeable concentration of individuals, in turn, created a substantial consumer base unlike anything England could have envisioned during the Middle Ages. During this period, England also witnessed the development of two major industries: clothing and mining. Furthermore, the discovery of the New Worlds tripled Europe's supply of gold and silver. Finally, the creation of an overseas trade market necessitated the invention of large financial centers that could distribute sizeable loans and capital to ambitious individuals or governments. Taken together these changes represented one of the largest economic transformations in the history of Western civilization.

As with any massive social reordering, the English economy's shift toward capitalism produced a clear set of winners and losers.

L.C. Knights observes, 'Not only were large commercial profits confined to a comparatively small section of the population...but those profits – and the financial conditions that made them possible – contributed to form a situation which aggravated poverty at the same time as it made it more conspicuous' (p. 55). One group, at least in Knights' view, that suffered as a result of the new economy was the artisans. In the Middle Ages, skilled craftsmen managed and owned the implements of their trade; however, in the Elizabethan-Jacobean economy, most became laborers who toiled under conditions determined by supervisors. Another loser was the landed aristocracy of the 15th and early 16th centuries. Long protected by the rigidity of the feudal system, these landowners gave way to a new class of men who 'owed their power not to the possession of land, like the old feudal nobility, nor to political-administrative talents, like the newer members of the Tudor aristocracy, but solely to their business ability' (Knights, p. 88). Many Englishmen resented these social climbers for their success and understandably so since their financial gain frequently came at the expense of someone else.

So how can these economic and social changes be seen generally in Jonson's writing and specifically in *Volpone*? Writing broadly about Jonson's work, Knights observes that 'Jonson is drawing on the anti-acquisitive tradition inherited from the Middle Ages' (p. 190). He then applies this to *Volpone*, noting that 'the comedy of *Volpone* is universal, but it would be perverse not to relate it to the acquisitiveness of a particular time and place' (p. 206). Thus, Knights casts Jonson as a moralist decrying the corrupt paths to affluence taken by many in the early 17th century. If one accepts Knights' opinion, then Jonson would belong to a large group of Englishmen who viewed the conspicuous consumption of the newly rich with great skepticism. In recent years Don Wayne has built upon Knights' understanding of Jonson; however, Wayne views Jonson not merely as a crusader against capitalist greed and corruption but also as a dramatist who is 'implicated in what he criticizes' (p. 28). Although Jonson objects to the individualism at the heart of nascent English capitalism and is nostalgic for the community-based approach of the Middle Ages, his success as a poet and playwright depends on self-assertion, a primary pillar of the new economy. The crux of Wayne's argument can be boiled down to the following statement:

> There is an interesting tension in Jonson's work between, on the one hand, the designation of rampant individualism as the origin of social disorder in Jacobean England, and, on the other, the poet's constant assertion of his own individuality and independence. (p. 29)

It should, however, be noted that even Wayne acknowledges *Volpone* is unique among Jonson's plays because it possesses a 'moral certitude' in its condemnation of acquisitiveness and unchecked individualism (p. 31).

Another scholar who sees *Volpone* as a commentary on the economic conditions of Jacobean England is Sean McEvoy. McEvoy points out that 'the amorality and theatricality of the free market are Jonson's subject in *Volpone*' and that 'all things [including a human being] can now be traded' (p. 55). McEvoy's sobering observation is a pointed reminder that every conversation between Volpone, Mosca, Voltore, Corbaccio and Corvino is exclusively transactional. Without the possibility of economic gain, there would be no reason for these men to communicate with each other. One can almost imagine them sitting silently in a room staring blankly at each other if money were not at stake. McEvoy's reading of the theatricality of the free market is just as insightful as his understanding of its amorality. He comments:

> In a free market economy unlimited self-transformation seem[s] possible.... Not only are the theatrical skills of Volpone and Mosca expertly deployed to maximum profit in the play, we also delight in self-transformation and performance which cannot be separated from the energy of capitalist accumulation, and which runs through this play like an electric charge. (p. 55)

In other words, a knack for disguise and an aptitude for performance are exceptionally valuable skills in a free market, and Volpone's and Mosca's mastery of these skills is what enables them to enrich their coffers. Thus, the newly available social mobility in the Jacobean economy can be thought of as a threat to the possibility of an authentic self because it encourages individuals to switch identities as often as it serves them in the business world.

Regardless of how one interprets *Volpone*, it is nearly impossible to deny that Jonson is using this play to ignite a conversation about the new economy and social order emerging in the Elizabethan-

Jacobean era. What exactly Jonson is trying to achieve by initiating this conversation is, of course, up to each reader to decide for him/herself.

Literary context

Jonson is a man both of and after his time. As a writer, he merges the popular forms of the early 17th century with the content, structure and tone of literature produced in Ancient Greece and Rome. As shown in the subsequent section on *Volpone*'s sources, Jonson appropriates and adapts an assortment of material from the Greco-Roman world, transforming it into something new and wholly unrecognizable; however, before delving into the specific works that *Volpone* makes use of, let us first examine three figures from antiquity – Horace, Aristophanes and Plautus – who supply the theoretical and practical framework for Jonson's drama.

As a treatise on the craft of poetry, Horace's *Ars Poetica* only lags behind Aristotle's *Poetics* in import; but when it comes to the plays of Ben Jonson, the long reach of Horace arguably extends beyond even that of Aristotle. Jonson's fixation with Horace is undeniable. He translated *Ars Poetica* as well as authored a commentary on the text. The former was published posthumously in 1640 while the latter was lost in a 1623 fire that destroyed a sizeable portion of Jonson's literary output. For Jonson the most important idea in *Ars Poetica* seems to have been its famous maxim that art should be both pleasurable and instructional. This is the ethical principle that guides almost all of Jonson's drama, and a paraphrasing of this precept even finds its way into the Prologue of *Volpone* when the speaker says, 'In all his poems still hath been this measure: / To mix profit with your pleasure' (ll. 7–8). While one may think that most works of literature adhere to this precept, such a belief would be misguided and easily disproven by the many Elizabethan and Jacobean plays that aim solely at merriment; thus, Jonson's strict adherence to this dictum imbues his work with a didacticism that is absent in the writing of many of his peers. Jonson also seems to have absorbed Horace's distinction between legitimate poetry and hack writing. In *Ars Poetica* Horace gives his unequivocal opinion of mediocrity in print:

A lawyer and pleader of middling rank falls short of the merit of eloquent Messalla, and knows not as much as Aulus Cascellius, yet he has a value. But that poets be of middling rank, neither men nor gods nor booksellers ever brooked. (p. 481)

Jonson echoes and embellishes this distinction in his Epistle to *Volpone* when he rails against practitioners of inferior poetry (or 'poetasters' as he calls them):

It is certain, nor can it with any forehead be opposed, that the too much licence of poetasters in this time hath much deformed their mistress, that every day their manifold and manifest ignorance doth stick unnatural reproaches upon her. But for their petulancy, it were an act of the greatest injustice either to let the learned suffer or so divine a skill (which indeed should not be attempted with unclean hands) to fall under the least contempt. (ll. 11–8)

And so what must be remembered when encountering Jonson's writing is the Horatian ambition of the man, for it is impossible to separate the content of Jonson's work from his views and aims.

Although the ideas of Horace offer a theoretical framework for Jonson's writing, the dramatic techniques developed by Aristophanes and Plautus, the two greatest comic playwrights from the classical era, provide Jonson with a practical template for building his plays. Jonson's debt to ancient comedy is even recognized by three different writers in the commendatory verses included in the 1607 Quarto of *Volpone*. The clearest of these acknowledgements comes from Dudley Diggs, who writes:

The strange new follies of this idle age,
In strange new forms, presented on the stage
By thy quick Muse, so pleased judicious eyes
That th'once-admirèd ancient comedy's
Fashions, like clothes grown out of fashion, lay
Locked up from use, until thy Fox birthday
In an old garb showed so much art and wit
As they the laurel gave to thee and it.
('To my good friend, Mr. Jonson', ll. 1–8)

Commenting generally on Jonson's debt to Aristophanic comedy, the modern scholar Coburn Gum asserts that Jonson's comedies share the following characteristics with the work of Aristophanes: a simple episodic structure with marginally connected events linked only by the wild schemes of the play's central characters, biting satires of living persons and a fascination with the vulgar and perverse. To Gum's list one could also add an aversion to domesticity on the stage. Speaking specifically about *Volpone*, Gum writes that 'the irony, broad humor, and inverted world of *Volpone* link it with Old Comedy' and that '*Volpone* is, above all, Aristophanic in its pitiless satire' (p. 159). Gum, however, does overreach in his analysis when he argues that Jonson's approach to characterization also derives from Aristophanes. Although there is certainly an overlap between the approaches of these two writers, it is much easier to see the similarities between Plautus' characters and Jonson's characters. Both Plautus and Jonson write almost exclusively about men whose entire beings are overrun by one trait (or 'humour' as Jonson terms it) while Aristophanes only periodically dramatizes such individuals. In the work of both Plautus and Jonson, a character's essence is whittled down to a lone characteristic, so much so that a person's name reflects his/her identity (Morose, Overdo, Surly, etc.). In *Volpone* these singular traits are embodied through the character's beastly essence. Thus, Jonson's mode of characterization is distinctly Plautine while his tone, setting and themes are Aristophanic.

Jonson's comedies, however, must be understood not only in conversation with Greco-Roman literature but with the comedies of the Elizabethan-Jacobean period as well. If there is one thing that defines English comedy during this period, it is that there is no easy way to define English comedy during this period. Unlike the comic traditions of Ancient Greece and Rome or Neoclassical France, English Renaissance comedy demonstrates little uniformity; instead, the comedies from this era are a mishmash of numerous comic forms. Despite the hybridity of English Renaissance comedy, it is still possible to place most comedies from this period in an appropriate subgenre so long as one also recognizes the limitations of these categorizations. In the 1590s the most popular of these subgenres was the romance. Romances written during this period share most or all of the following characteristics: a plot centered around lovers overcoming a series of obstacles to their union, a rural or idyllic location far removed from city life, a prominent role for magic in the narrative and a story that traverses a large amount of time and space. Toward the end of the 16th century, this style of comedy fell out of fashion, and Londoners clamored for a new comic form (later dubbed City Comedy by scholars) that more closely resembled their own experiences. Coincidentally, it was just around this time that Ben Jonson was making his way into the English theater. The match between the changing tastes of the public and the prodigious talents of the man could not have been more perfect.

As Brian Gibbons notes, 'Jonson fathered the genre [of City Comedy], powerfully shaped its growth and crowned its maturity' (p. 18). Gibbons goes on to elucidate the central characteristics of City Comedy, saying the following:

> We might define the genre City Comedy, then, by the fact that the plays are all satiric and have urban settings, with characters and incident appropriate to such settings; they exclude material appropriate to romance, fairy tale, sentimental legend or patriotic chronicle. (p. 24)

Gibbons' definition, especially the portion dealing with what City Comedy excludes, proves quite useful when thinking about Jonson's comedies. If anything, Jonson is more concerned with what his plays are not than with what they are. His comedies, especially his four middle comedies written between 1606 and 1614 (*Volpone*, *Epicene*, *The Alchemist* and *Bartholomew Fair*), are a revolt against romance and other forms of love-centered comedy. Jonson's middle comedies scoff at the very idea of eternal union. *Volpone* concludes with the presumed dissolution of the warped marriage between Corvino and Celia, and the climax of his next play, *Epicene*, is the revelation that the marriage between Morose and the titular character is null and void because Epicene, like 'her' husband, is a man. During a time when almost all comedies concluded with a marriage, it is difficult to imagine a more forceful protest against such a convention. Jonson's distaste for magic and the supernatural is equally pronounced. In stark contrast to the miraculous interventions of fairies and magicians, Jonson's characters create their own magic, relying solely on guile and disguise to bring their plans to fruition. Through the triumph of their wit, they testify to the power of self-reliance, a trait that is frequently absent or diminished in the heroes and heroines of romantic comedy. Finally, Jonson rejects the sprawling narratives so typical of romance. All four of Jonson's middle comedies take place in one city over a 24-hour period. (*The Alchemist* even takes place in one house.) Clearly the fact that Jonson's middle comedies are the very antithesis of romance is more than just coincidence. It is an indicator that Jonson is keenly aware of the literary landscape and that he is consciously revolting against the dominant form of the 1590s in an effort to kill it.

Sources

The most erudite playwright of his era, Jonson's encyclopedic knowledge of classical and medieval literature is nothing short of astounding. Even more remarkable, though, is his knack for transforming that knowledge into unique dramatic creations. Some critics argue that Jonson's attachment to his source material goes too far at times, especially when he showcases his scholarship at the expense of plot and character development. These complaints are not without merit, and Jonson's lesser work is certainly rife with examples of excess erudition. *Volpone*, by and large, has rightfully escaped this charge. The play, while it is indebted to a variety of sources, refrains from taking excessive detours into Jonson's personal library. *Volpone* is shaped by two kinds of sources: classical texts about legacy hunters and beast fables. For the legacy-hunting narrative, Jonson uses Horace's *Satires*, Petronius' *The Satyricon* and Lucian's *Dialogues of the Dead*; and for animal lore, he pulls from the fables of Aesop and William Caxton's translation of *The History of Reynard the Fox*. In all five instances, a reader familiar with the source material can see its influence on the play's plot and characters; nevertheless, the effect is subtle, allowing Jonson's originality still to shine through.

In Horace's *Satires*, Ulysses (a.k.a. Odysseus) enters the underworld and asks the prophet Tiresias how he can recover his lost fortune. Fragments of Tiresias' cynical answer in which he suggests that Ulysses take up the practice of legacy hunting can be seen sprinkled throughout *Volpone*. Two passages, though, are especially pertinent:

> If some day a case, great or small, be contested in the Forum, whichever of the parties is rich and childless, villain though he be, who with wanton impudence calls the better man into court, do you become his advocate; spurn the citizen of the better name and cause. (p. 201)

And:

> Is he a libertine? See that he has not to ask you; yourself obligingly hand over Penelope [i.e., your wife] to your better. (p. 205)

In the first passage, one can see the prototype for Voltore, who becomes Volpone's advocate in his case against the virtuous Bonario and Celia; and the second passage lays the foundation for Corvino's prostitution of his wife in an effort to win Volpone's affection.

In contrast to *Satires*, which focuses on those who make their fortune by ingratiating themselves to wealthy men who are childless, *The Satyricon* looks at the exploits of those who feign sickness in an effort to attract gifts from overeager legacy hunters. A group of men arrive in Croton, an Italian town known for its insatiable legacy hunters; and one of the men in the group, Eumolpus, concocts a scheme in which he poses as a dying millionaire who has recently lost his only son while everyone else in the group pretends to be his slaves. The whole plot is carried out and spoken of as if it were a play. This notion that confidence games are a form of theater appears frequently in *Volpone* and is the driving force behind the play's persistent metatheatricality. In addition to appropriating Petronius' view of confidence games, Jonson seems to have made the following description of Croton the model for his fictionalized Venice:

> In that town literature and the arts go utterly unhonored; eloquence there has no prestige; and those who live the good and simple life find no admirers. Any man you meet in that town you may be certain belongs to one of two classes: the makers of wills and those who pursue the makers of wills. You will find no fathers there, for those with natural heirs of their own are regarded as pariahs.... In short, sirs, you are going to a place which is like a countryside ravaged by the plague, a place in which you will see only two things: the bodies of those who are eaten, and the carrion crows who eat them. (pp. 132–3)

A couple of items in this passage are readily apparent in *Volpone*, mainly the view that fatherhood and family are antithetical to the pursuit of wealth (a view that Volpone espouses quite often and Corbaccio and Corvino demonstrate through their actions) and the utter lack of regard for human decency as evidenced by the ways in which the greedy cannibalize each other. (Crow also connects with Corvino, whose name translates as 'black like a crow' and whom Volpone refers to as a 'carrion crow'.)

Similar to Petronius' *The Satyricon*, Lucian's *Dialogues of the Dead* shows how wily men posing as invalids can gull conniving legacy hunters. The fate of one such legacy hunter, Cnemon, greatly resembles that of Corbaccio after he disinherits Bonario. Cnemon complains:

> I've been outsmarted, poor fool that I am, and have left an heir I didn't want, passing over those I'd have preferred to have my property.... I'd been showering my attentions on Hermolaus, the childless millionaire, in hopes of his death, and he was glad enough to have them. So I thought of another clever move, and decided to make my will public. I've left him all my property in it, hoping he in turn would emulate me, and do the same by me. (p. 93)

In contrast to Cnemon is Polystratus, Lucian's nonagenarian con man. Gloating in the afterlife, Polystratus happily proclaims:

> I was almost worshipped by them [i.e., legacy hunters]. Often I would be coy, and occasionally bar my door to some of them, but they would vie with each other in their zeal for my affection.... I would keep saying in public that I had left each of them as my heir, and each would believe me and show himself more assiduous than ever in his flattery; but all the time my real will was different and I left them instructions to go to the devil one and all. (p. 99)

It is almost impossible not to see the echo of this in Volpone's early manipulation of the legacy hunters and in his subsequent mockery of them when Mosca is proclaimed the heir. Thus, these three works, when taken together, provide Jonson with the template for his legacy hunters and masquerading invalid.

Jonson then layers his all-too-human tale of greed and legacy hunting with a series of beast fables. The genius of *Volpone* is that it is simultaneously a quasi-realistic look at city life in the early 1600s and an allegorical tale grounded in a diverse body of animal lore. It is a play about men and beasts, or more precisely it is a play about men who behave like beasts. More than three centuries before George Orwell's concluding observation in *Animal Farm* that man and animal can no longer be differentiated, Jonson makes the same point; and he does it by connecting the characters and incidents in his play to the fables of Aesop and the medieval epic about Reynard the Fox.

Volpone's connection to Aesop's *Fables* is loose yet evident. Jonson clearly pulls characteristics of Aesop's animals and reproduces them in his characters. This is especially true of Volpone (an old fox) and Mosca (a fly). There are three Aesopian tales ('The Fox with a Swollen Stomach', 'The Fox and the Huge Serpent' and 'The Flies') in which either a fox or fly gorges or stretches himself to the point of self-annihilation. In all three fables, these animals, similar to Volpone and Mosca, are undone by their inability to moderate their appetites. There are also two stories ('The Raven and the Fox' and 'The Tortoise and the Eagle') whose events are faintly visible in *Volpone*. In the former, a fox outwits a raven (Corbaccio), making off with his food (for a direct reference to this fable in the play see V.viii); and in the latter, a tortoise (Sir Pol), desperate to fly, is dropped to his death by an oversized bird (Peregrine). Although none of these five fables plays a substantive role in the narrative of *Volpone*, one must still acknowledge their reverberations, especially for the many in Jonson's audience who were intimately familiar with popular animal lore.

For a more direct correspondence, it is useful to consult William Caxton's 1481 translation of *The History of Reynard the Fox*. Tales of the devilish fox Reynard first cropped up in Europe in the 12th century, and in subsequent centuries these stories took many forms, both written and oral. Originating in France, the figure of Reynard was popularized by two Flemish verse epics written in the 13th and 14th centuries. In 1479 these verse epics were rendered into a more readable prose version by an anonymous Dutch author. Caxton then translated this prose version into English in 1481; and it is Caxton's translation, scholars believe, that Jonson consulted as he worked on *Volpone* although there are some who theorize that Jonson was also familiar with the Dutch versions since he did his military service in Flanders. R.B. Parker, who has written extensively about the connection between Caxton's *Reynard* and Jonson's *Volpone*, identifies several points of intersection:

the two trials of Reynard/the court proceedings against Volpone, Reynard's feigning death/Volpone's false sickness, Reynard's disguise as a doctor/Volpone's disguise as the mountebank and Reynard as a musician/Volpone as a singing seducer of Celia. Although Parker focuses primarily on the trials, the most obvious parallel is that of the fox feigning death, which can be found in chapter 24 of *The History of Reynard the Fox*. In this chapter, titled 'How Corbant the Rook Complained on the Fox for the Death of His Wife', Reynard plays dead before entrapping and devouring Corbant's wife. Even though the story lacks a carnal element (it is worth mentioning that the beast epic does contain other stories of Reynard committing sexual assault), its primary image of the false fox playing sick to ensnare a carrion crow and his wife is central to the narrative of *Volpone*. The connection between beast fables and *Volpone*, though, should not be thought of merely as an academic exercise done for Jonson's own amusement. The relationship has both a practical application and interpretive implication, for as Parker observes:

> The original staging may well have recalled some of the most familiar scenes of the widespread fox iconography; at all events, it would have been less likely for the staging to present men with some characteristics of animals – as has been the tendency in modern productions – and more likely for it to follow beast-epic convention and present the characters as recognizable animals who behave like men. (p. 42)

On an interpretative level, Jonson's use of allegorical animal lore advances his objective of stripping *Volpone* of moral ambiguity. This is especially true regarding his use of Caxton's *Reynard*, which locates the play in a medieval world of virtue and vice. Should the authorities have questioned Jonson about the play's meaning, he easily could have pointed to his appropriation of these morality tales and explained that *Volpone* is part of the same tradition.

Thus, it should be apparent that Jonson's manipulation of source material is about much more than showcasing his scholarship although that certainly is a motivating factor. Jonson utilizes a diverse array of sources to stimulate his creativity, to make his plays more heterogeneous, to inform staging choices and to shape the interpretation of his work.

3 Commentary

Prologue[1]

1 to the end It is not very often that a play begins without the playwright identifying the speaker of the first line, but it is also not very often that a playwright like Ben Jonson comes along. Known for flouting convention while simultaneously touting his adherence to the rules of classical drama, Jonson is a paradox of reverence and irreverence, rule abiding and rule breaking; and this contradiction is on full display in the prologue. The open-ended nature of the first speech (if it is even preserved in performance) leaves a director with numerous options and questions when thinking about how best to begin the production. Most importantly, a director must select the appropriate actor(s) to deliver the prologue. Looking at the meter, several scholars have observed that the verse sounds strikingly similar to the verse of Nano, Androgyno and Castrone. Another option would be to assign the prologue to the actor portraying Volpone. This choice lends the production a nice symmetry since it is Volpone who delivers the epilogue. It is also possible for a director to enlist multiple speakers and divide the text among some or all of the cast members, creating a unified show of support for Jonson's claim of literary superiority. The director must also decide whether s/he wishes to present the speaker(s) as actor(s) or character(s). Having the speech delivered by performers in street clothes creates a very different experience for the audience than a prologue that is spoken by costumed actors adopting the personas of their characters. Although both approaches yield dynamic staging possibilities, it seems from the personal nature of the prologue that Jonson

---

[1] All line divisions are taken from Brian Parker's revised Manchester University Press edition.

intends for the opening of *Volpone*, in contrast to the role-playing and theatrics that dominate the play, to be blunt and devoid of theatrical adornments.

Tonally, too, this speech presents a director with an interesting paradox. On the one hand, the speech is bookish. It extols Aristotelian theory and advocates for poetry with substance. On the other hand, it is brash and confrontational. It accuses Jonson's rivals of lacking originality and skill. It boasts of Jonson's ability to complete *Volpone* in a mere five weeks, and its final couplet makes the brazen claim that the audience will still be laughing a week later despite the play's strict adherence to the dictums of classical drama. This tension between comedy, which is transgressive in nature, and the neoclassical ideal, which reduces drama to a series of codes, is at the heart of *Volpone*; and Jonson clearly wants his audience to believe from the outset that these two diametrically opposed forces can coexist. Any production must prove him right.

Act I

Act I, scene i

1–27 Before diving into the opening lines of *Volpone*, it is necessary to consider how the stage might look. The entirety of the first act as well as substantial portions of the third and fifth acts take place inside Volpone's house; therefore, it is important for the reader to be able to envision possibilities for the set design. A good set design should supply the audience with information about Volpone's lifestyle and daily existence, connect Volpone's physical environment to his psychology and express several of the play's central themes. One way to do this is to overpopulate the space with golden objects and possessions. *Volpone*, the play, is a critique of excess; and Volpone, the character, is the embodiment of unchecked greed and acquisitiveness. The design must physicalize these traits and ideas, perhaps so much so that the characters struggle to maneuver through the maze of riches that will eventually entrap them. One object, in particular, is worthy of special attention: Volpone's bed. Because so much of the play's action takes place in and around his bed, this set piece needs to be in a prominent, accessible location. It also must be sizeable enough to accommodate much of the stage business and physical comedy that occurs throughout the play.

As for the text, it opens with Volpone proclaiming, 'Good morning to the day!' There are not many plays that begin more optimistically than this. When he awakes, Volpone is all anticipation, eager to begin his knavery and indulge his cunning. Of course, the audience at this point knows nothing about the quality of the man who has so joyfully greeted the morn. In all likelihood, they assume the best about a fellow so chipper at dawn. At least they do until Volpone completes the first line by saying, 'And next, my gold!' It is a shocking statement. Not only does it defy the expectation set in the first half of the line, but it is an affront to one of the most sacred practices of the period: giving thanks to God upon arising. So monomaniacal is Volpone's obsession that immediately after regaining consciousness he begs audience with his riches. He even co-opts the language of faith, calling the casing for his gold a 'shrine' and his treasure the 'world's soul'. For almost 30 lines he continues in this vein, esteeming gold over the sun, valuing wealth more than family and equating riches with virtue. The speech is so over-the-top that it is hard not to envision Volpone kissing (which he asks to do in line 11), fondling and bathing in his booty. As an audience member, one might even begin to wonder if there will be an end to Volpone's speech or if the entire play will be an uninterrupted paean to wealth, which it would be if Mosca, who has presumably grown quite impatient with his master's daily devotional, were not present to interrupt the sacrilege.

28–70 Mosca's interruption inaugurates an exercise in self-justification, as the two men define who they are by listing what they are not. The exchange is revealing, for it shows that neither Mosca nor Volpone considers himself to be a villain. Both of them see honor in how they have attained and used their wealth. Perhaps the two men merely say these things so that they can sleep at night, but it seems more likely that these sentiments genuinely reflect their belief that the swindle is a true art, more noble than the honest professions of farming or butchery. When Volpone says that he glories 'more in the cunning purchase of [his] wealth than in the glad possession', he admits a fundamental truth about himself: he is addicted to the chase, and no amount of gold can sate him because it is the game, not the prize, that excites him.

This interaction between Volpone and Mosca is important for another reason as well: it helps lay the groundwork for the relationship that will unfold over the course of the play. At the heart of *Volpone* is the connection between the magnifico and his parasite, so it is hardly happenstance that Jonson opens his comedy with a scene featuring these two men. Their relationship in the early moments of the play can be interpreted and staged several ways. It can be adversarial. This view is supported by the fact that every speech in this beat, whether it belongs to Volpone or Mosca, is cut off by an interruption from the other character. The interruptions make it appear as if the two men are actors competing for stage time, almost like a Jacobean rendition of Irving Berlin's 'Anything You Can Do'; however, there is also a danger in making Volpone and Mosca outwardly competitive with each other at such an early juncture in the play. Although a little foreshadowing is a good thing, too much foreshadowing can kill suspense and render a production unnecessarily static. Another possibility is to make Mosca overly sycophantic toward Volpone. This view would result in a Mosca who shamelessly boosts his master's ego with lies designed to elicit small tokens of affection. One final option is to treat Volpone and Mosca as equals, partners with compatible personalities and shared interests. By presenting the duo as comrades, this approach maximizes the dramatic payoff that comes from the subsequent dissolution of their relationship; however, it also runs the risk of glossing over the early signs of Mosca's discontent with his master.

70 to the end After Mosca exits to retrieve Volpone's entertainment (a dwarf, a eunuch and a fool), Volpone, perhaps musing to himself or perhaps addressing the audience, asks a most revealing question: 'What should I do?' More than any other malady, Volpone suffers from perpetual ennui, and it is this condition that will eventually prove his undoing. He is incapable of remaining idle. One of the great ironies in the figure of Volpone is that the man who plays dead for a living cannot bear to be still. It is essential that any actor playing the kinetic Volpone keep this in mind. During this monologue, Volpone also sets the stage for the treachery that is to come. By having Volpone declare his plans, Jonson makes the audience complicit in the double-cross. They are aware that a defrauding is about to take place; and like Volpone awaiting the performance of his three freaks, they eagerly anticipate the theatrical gamesmanship and crimes about to occur.

Act I, scene ii

1–81 A frequent casualty in the cutting room, the freaks' first interlude presents three problems for contemporary productions: its obscure references to Pythagoras' theories on the transmigration of souls are unlikely to excite the interests of a 21st-century audience, it unnecessarily interrupts what is an otherwise taut first act focused on the duping of the three legacy hunters and it poses serious difficulties for productions trying to achieve a unified performance style. Regarding the first problem, there is not a great solution unless one wants to rewrite the text. Some productions have opted for a dumb show since this preserves the freaks' aesthetic and thematic contribution while avoiding their arcane text. It is also possible to shift the focus away from the content of the text and draw the audience's attention almost exclusively to its singsong style, thereby turning the words into utter nonsense. Either way, it is inevitable that the meaning of the original text will need to be deemphasized for a modern audience.

As for the structural critique, it is a valid one. If one expects a version of *Volpone* with a straightforward trajectory that tracks only the machinations of Volpone and Mosca, then it is difficult to see this skit as anything other than an interruption of the play's central action. Searching for a reason why Jonson might have included this detour, some scholars have theorized that it was added to the university productions at Oxford and Cambridge as a showcase for Jonson's erudition. Others have claimed that Jonson inserted Nano, Androgyno and Castrone into the play to please James I, who had a twisted fascination with deformities. Although these hypotheses may be historically accurate, they still reflect a belief that these characters and their antics are alien to the play. Such a reading oversimplifies Jonson's work. The freaks' performance is not so much an interruption as it is a ceremonial inauguration of the play's action. Their meditation on reincarnation can be seen as a celebration of transformation, and their musical tribute to foolery is a way of praising performance and role-playing. When we see Volpone in the first scene, he is himself. Immediately following the freaks' performance,

Volpone transforms into someone else; and he, like a soul moving from host to host, never stops transforming until his uncasing in the final scene. Is it a coincidence that all this happens after the freaks' routine?

The final difficulty presented by Nano, Androgyno and Castrone is that of style. Three centuries before the formal advent of expressionism, the freaks' grotesque physiognomy serves as a physical embodiment of the upside-down moral and sexual universe that all the characters inhabit. The tremendous advantage of this is that it brings an air of modernity to a play that is more than four centuries old and frequently derided as excessively classical; nevertheless, the presence of the freaks raises several questions: Where do these characters fit in the landscape of the play? Is their grotesquerie self-contained, or does it manifest itself in other staging and character choices throughout the production? Although it is possible to treat the interludes of Nano, Androgyno and Castrone as radical breaks from reality, this has the potential to lead to a disjointed experience for viewers. This is not inherently negative, but it does result in a production that is more a collection of disparate parts than the unified whole Jonson claims *Volpone* to be. A more integrated approach would incorporate the freaks and all that they embody into every aspect of the production. This may mean that Nano, Androgyno and Castrone silently appear as onlookers throughout the production and not only in the places where Jonson has scripted an entrance for them. It may also require other characters to adopt certain grotesque attributes, which should not be overly difficult if a production has already decided to emphasize the bestial nature of the characters. In short, the freaks have much to offer modern productions of *Volpone*; however, they must be used in a way that is accessible to contemporary audiences, and their role in the action, be it as a grotesque sideshow or emblems of the play's moral universe, must be carefully considered.

82 to the end What is remarkable about the final 46 lines of this scene is all that has to happen in such a short time frame. This beat should not last more than a minute and a half, yet by its end Volpone has physically changed from a spry gentleman into a grotesque invalid. The more sizeable the metamorphosis, the more the audience will appreciate the talents of Volpone and Mosca. This moment is extremely metatheatrical, as the actor playing Volpone (a character who also happens to be an actor) changes his costume in full view of the audience. From the text we know that at minimum Volpone must wrap himself in furs, put on a nightcap and cloud his eyes with ointment; however, this barely scratches the surface of the ginormous transformation effected by Volpone. Some of these changes go beyond costumes and makeup and must be manifest in Volpone's physicality. The list of maladies enumerated in lines 124–5 gives insight into what will be required of Volpone. The two primary symptoms of these diseases are respiratory distress and muscular degeneration, so it is imperative that Volpone radically alter his voice and maneuver his body in a spastic, uncontrolled manner throughout the visits of the legacy hunters. The stranger his voice and the more ridiculous his movements, the more likely it is that the audience will find humor in the situation.

Easy to lose sight of during Volpone's chaotic costume change is Mosca. As he often does, Mosca skillfully recedes into the background, humbly preparing his star for the ensuing performance; however, Mosca says something quite revealing in lines 98–109. In contrast to Volpone, who is motivated by ennui and the pursuit of wealth, Mosca is animated by a sadistic impulse. While Volpone delights in the gifts he is about to receive from Voltore, Mosca just laughs strangely. It has the potential to be a discomfiting moment. When a puzzled Volpone questions him about this, Mosca confesses that he is amused by Voltore's misplaced self-satisfaction and that he takes great delight in the inevitable suffering and shaming that will ensue when Voltore's designs fail to come to fruition. Thus, we see early on that Mosca is more sinister than his playful and restless master.

Act I, scene iii

1–30 The first half of this scene belongs to Volpone. He lives out the fantasy of almost all aspiring actors when he plays a man on his deathbed. Of course, it is not so much a deathbed scene as it is a parody of one. His last words to Voltore resemble every hackneyed line uttered by a character departing this world in a fit of melodrama. How can one not chuckle at the phrases 'I am sailing to my port' and 'I am glad I am so near my haven'? The only thing that could make Volpone's performance more over-the-top would be interrupting his lines with wheezing fits or death rattles, so Jonson makes sure to include those as well, scripting the final two iambs of lines 28 and 29 as choking noises. For an actor playing Volpone, this sequence is comic gold. The audience is already delighted by the dramatic irony of the situation, and Volpone's hamming only adds to their pleasure. The challenge in performance, however, is finding that elusive balance between self-conscious theatricality and plausibility. The actor playing Volpone cannot be so histrionic that he loses all credibility as a competent performer, but he cannot be so naturalistic that he removes all joy and playfulness from the scene.

The other extraordinary aspect of this beat is that Voltore is oblivious to the artificiality of the entire spectacle. One has to wonder if it is because he is naturally obtuse or if he is so consumed with being named Volpone's heir that he fails to see what is obviously in front of him. Given Voltore's own abilities as a con artist, the latter reading seems more likely. Voltore, however, will not be the last character who lets himself see what he wants to see rather than what is plain to see. In other words, the legacy hunters are not so much deceived by others as they are by their own desires. The secret of Volpone and Mosca's con is that they are selling people something they already believe in: the possibility of becoming fabulously wealthy.

31 to the end   It is unclear whether Volpone's concluding line at 30 is a signal to Mosca that he should take over the scene or if Mosca, weary of his master's histrionics, wrests control of the situation with a testy, 'Well, we must all go.' Either way, it is undeniable that the second half of the scene belongs to Mosca. As much as Volpone toys with Voltore during the first 30 lines, Mosca exerts twice as much control in the ensuing 48 lines. His manipulation is nothing short of masterful. By humbling himself before Voltore, he gives Voltore a feeling of power; and by praising Voltore's virtue, he gives Voltore a false sense of righteousness. Few things make a man more content than feeling strong and virtuous, and Mosca clearly knows how to make Voltore believe that he is both. Yet Mosca does all this with a bitter irony, cleverly inserting unnoticed digs at Voltore and his profession. Even the unexpected knock at line 66 is a gift to Mosca, who directs Voltore to leave with a sullen expression. This makes the next visitor, Corbaccio, more likely to believe that he is the sole heir and allows Voltore the satisfaction of playing a role in the deception of some other poor fool. This will be a recurrent idea throughout the text, as each legacy hunter delights in thinking that he alone is special and that the other legacy hunters are nothing more than suckers done in by their own stupidity. The irony is delicious and a hallmark of Jonson's middle comedies.

Despite his silence for the remainder of the scene with Voltore, Volpone is still a significant presence on stage. Does he simply lie motionless in bed and impersonate an unconscious man? Does he continue to pursue the limelight by making gratuitous sounds of dying? Does he periodically break character to get a glimpse of his disciple giving a virtuoso performance? Although there is no clear or correct answer, one thing is certain: Volpone seems to get more joy from watching Mosca than he does from performing. As soon as Voltore exits, Volpone leaps to his feet and makes to kiss his servant. Only Corbaccio's arrival and Mosca's terse rejection stay Volpone's physical affection. It is a strange moment to behold, and it is the first sign that the play's ostensible star might just be a supporting character in Mosca's drama.

Act I, scene iv

1–132 50 lines longer than both the previous scene with Voltore and the subsequent scene with Corvino, Corbaccio's visit is notable for more than just its length. It is probably the most humorous and certainly the most tense of the three encounters with the legacy hunters. For this reason some productions and early editors transpose this scene with the following scene, thereby making it the climax of the first act. Although this editorial choice raises significant problems, mainly that it separates the launching point for the second act (Mosca convincing Volpone to pursue Corvino's wife) from the central plot point of the second act (Volpone's pursuit of Celia), it does demonstrate a recognition that this scene contains a danger that is lacking in the two scenes that bookend it. From where does this danger arise? From Mosca's request that Corbaccio disinherit his son. This is the first time in the play that one of Volpone's suitors must forfeit more than money to advance his cause. Corbaccio must either jeopardize his relationship with his son to stay in Volpone's good graces or give up his hope of winning Volpone's treasure. One way to think of this situation is as a poker game. Mosca has upped the ante, and Corbaccio must decide whether he wishes to stay in the hand or walk away. By putting his son into the kitty, Corbaccio significantly increases his investment in the game, thus making it more difficult for him to fold later even if he starts to suspect that he might have a losing hand. Corbaccio is not unique in this regard, as all the characters at some point in the play make increasingly risky and desperate decisions in the vain hope that they can recoup prior losses. As with most gamblers, this recklessness only causes the legacy hunters to lose even more. Mosca, of course, does this not because he and Volpone need to enlarge their wealth with Corbaccio's inheritance but because he wants to see how much he can get other people to sacrifice. This scene's bounty is a child. Still to come are one's wife, one's manhood and one's professional integrity.

Despite the cruelty of this scene, it is delightfully funny. Corbaccio's inability to hear Mosca brings about a series of comic misunderstandings while simultaneously adding to the irony of Corbaccio's ambitions. It almost seems wrong to be amused by Corbaccio's genuine infirmities (and some early critics have said as much, criticizing Jonson for poking fun of a man who could not help his physical condition), but the humor of his deafness and the extent of his stupidity are too strong to ignore. How can one not laugh at Corbaccio convincing himself that he is the originator of the plot to disinherit his son? However, as with most humor, there is a certain amount of pathos involved. Similar to Volpone and Mosca, Corbaccio is not really motivated by money. Rather he needs this inheritance to feel young again. 'I may ha' my youth restored to me', he says in the false hope that outliving Volpone and acquiring his fortune will somehow prove that he is not of the dying age. So powerful is his desire to put off death that he will risk anything, even his relationship with his son, to prolong the illusion that he is still young and in the game.

And where is Volpone during all of this? Lying silently on the bed, written out of the play that he fancied himself the star of.

132 to the end   As with the previous scene, Volpone is again unable to restrain his affection for Mosca after witnessing another of his masterful performances. This time, however, the kiss or embrace appears to be consummated. Whether Mosca receives this token of Volpone's affections gracefully or begrudgingly says a great deal about how comfortable Mosca is with being openly disdainful of his master. It is quite possible that Mosca never stops humoring Volpone for even a moment, but it is also possible that Volpone's immaturity and exuberance disgust the methodical Mosca so much that he cannot conceal his contempt. Certainly, the actor playing Mosca has an interesting choice to make when his character is faced with an unwanted advance. As for Volpone, this will not be the last time in the play that he makes a forceful advance at a character. What might be motivating these outbursts of affection? It seems that he has a problem with self-control. He allows himself to become so excited that he cannot keep his passions in check. Like many actors, Volpone experiences emotions on a deeper level than the average human, and this leads to erratic, impulsive and over-the-top behavior.

Line 138 in this beat is especially noteworthy: Volpone says, 'I never knew thee in so rare a humour.' Is it simply that Volpone does not accurately recall Mosca's talent and achievements, or is there something different about Mosca on this day? Perhaps he has known all along that today would be the day when he betrays his master, and that is why his performance is inspired and invigorated in ways that it had not been previously. At the very least, it is logical to assume that something is new about Mosca's behavior, if only for the reason that it is more dramatically compelling when this day and these interactions are irregular events and not everyday occurrences.

Act I, scene v

1–82 The last of the three legacy hunters, Corvino, is a sadist like Mosca. The similarities between the two men lead to a remarkable comic sequence in which both Mosca and Corvino holler insults into the ostensibly deaf ear of Volpone. This is yet another early example of Mosca subverting his master's authority and using Volpone's disguise as an invalid against him. Despite the hints of rebellion, this scene is all fun and games because Corvino shows himself as a man whose sadism has its limit. Unlike Corbaccio, who comes armed with a poisoned pill, Corvino will not have Volpone's blood on his hands even after Mosca urges him toward it. Just as he does with Corbaccio, Mosca wants to gauge the limits of Corvino's depravity; and Corvino's limit is playing an active role in murder. When Mosca questions Corvino about his sudden pang of conscience, Corvino is at a loss to explain his hesitation. It is one of the few moments in the play in which a character encounters a line that he will not cross, and it is confusing and surprising for all involved. Corvino's visit ends rather abruptly and awkwardly after Mosca inappropriately mentions Corvino's wife. The remark immediately triggers Corvino's jealousy, and he races home to make sure that his wife has not been unfaithful in his absence. It is a wonderful foreshadowing of what is to come in the next act.

83 to the end   Just as he does with Corbaccio, Mosca slyly embeds an idea in Volpone's mind and lets it run its inevitable course. Knowing just the right buttons to push, Mosca tempts Volpone by likening Celia to gold, and he continues to pique Volpone's interest by making seemingly casual references to Celia's unattainability. Each additional remark about the difficulties of wooing Celia only serves to whet Volpone's appetite for this mystery woman. By the time Mosca is done dangling the forbidden fruit, Volpone is ready to launch himself full throttle into this perilous situation. The question is what is motivating Mosca. Is he simply in search of a new adventure after growing bored with the old routine? Is he indulging his sadistic impulse at Corvino's expense, or is this the first move in his plan to trap Volpone? Mosca is undoubtedly the orchestrator of events in the play. He can be thought of as a playwright, meticulously plotting and arranging each sequence; however, as every playwright knows, sometimes situations do not play out as they have been diagrammed: characters make unexpected decisions, new elements come into play and the story takes unanticipated turns. This is the first juncture in the play in which it is impossible to proceed without intense consideration of the plot that Mosca, as playwright, is devising. What is he intending to accomplish by sending Volpone after Corvino's wife? And as we read further, we must consider which events in the ensuing acts are part of Mosca's master plan and which are the unintended consequences of a scheme that has gone awry. One's answers to these questions will have far-reaching implications in production, for they will ultimately determine how the actor portraying Mosca responds to the proliferation of complications throughout the remainder of the play. Although there is not a 'correct' way to approach each of the complications, it is essential that the actor always make it clear to the audience when Mosca is improvising and when he is following a carefully constructed script.

Act II

Act II, scene i

1 to the end   Act I of *Volpone* is constructed with an almost surgical precision. With great economy Jonson introduces the play's two central figures and establishes their relationship with the play's major supporting characters. In addition, Jonson does a superb job of setting the stage for a second act that will center around Volpone's pursuit of Corvino's wife, so it is more than a little surprising to see two very out of place Englishmen conversing on the stage at the start of Act II. What are they doing in Venice? What are they doing in this play? For a playwright who adheres so meticulously to the unity of time (the dictum that a play's action must not exceed one day) and the unity of place (the rule that a play's action must take place in only one location), Jonson shows a strange disregard for the unity of action (the idea that all scenes in the play should grow out of one central story). Messy subplots consistently triumph over the neoclassical desire for order in Jonson's plays. That being said, Peregrine and Sir Pol initially seem so out of place that it is reasonable to wonder if Jonson inserted these two characters simply to appease two clamorous company members in the King's Men demanding substantial roles in the play; or perhaps Jonson, against his own wishes, cowed to the tastes of Jacobean theatergoers and gave them what they wanted: a comic British subplot full of buffoonery to offset the more serious tale of Venetian intrigue. It is also possible that Jonson had serious artistic reasons for including this British detour. Although no one can reasonably argue that Sir Pol and Peregrine are a central part of the play's action, echoes of the play's primary narrative of manipulation and humiliation can be seen in the subplot as well. The stakes are lower, but the shame is no less real. Even still, the subplot in *Volpone* presents a major structural problem. Its closest analogue is the *intermezzo* of the Italian theater and opera. *Intermezzi* take place between the acts and distract the audience with comedy and spectacle. Despite lacking the spectacle of its Italian analogue, the three episodes featuring Sir Pol and Peregrine, like the *intermezzi*, can be conceived of as a separate and freestanding work that interrupts the high-stakes central narrative with a diversionary dramatization of low-stakes trickery. In this way it functions as a much needed palate cleanser for some while for others it appears to be an unnecessary distraction and momentum killer. So what is a director or dramaturg to do? The truth is that there is not a perfect solution. Productions that leave the subplot untouched are almost invariably criticized for their length and plodding pace; however, those productions that excise the Sir Pol plotline typically leave critics with a nagging sense that the evening is somehow incomplete. One can split the difference and offer a skeletal version of the subplot, but even a little trimming can add to the seeming randomness of these events, making audience members wonder all the more about their inclusion in the first place. Ultimately, what a director decides to do with the subplot depends on the larger aims of the production. A production in search of efficiency and dramatic momentum will likely discard most or all of the Sir Pol scenes while a production that wants to explore all of the play's quirks and unique features will almost certainly preserve the Sir Pol scenes[2].

Although I am predisposed toward economy in production, particularly given the dwindling attention span of today's audience, we will move forward with the assumption that these scenes are to be performed in their entirety since that is how they appear in the published text of the play. As we approach these scenes, it will be useful to consider ways of unlocking their dramatic potential. To do this we must think about the arc of the Sir Pol-Peregrine relationship. Where does it start, where does it end, and how does something that begins so benignly end so cruelly? At the beginning of II.i, Peregrine is simply puzzled by Sir Pol's almost unfathomable ignorance; however, as the scene progresses, Peregrine comes to realize that Sir Pol is even stupider than he first appears. This recognition coincides with a steady increase in the ridiculousness of Sir Pol's comments, which culminate in his ludicrous claim that a recently deceased local fool was a high-level government agent who received state secrets smuggled in cabbages. By the conclusion of their conversation, Peregrine has come to view Sir Pol as a never-ending source of

---

[2] For a spirited defense of the Sir Pol subplot see Jonas Barish, 'The Double Plot in *Volpone*', *Modern Philology*, 51:2 (1953), pp. 83-92.

amusement, and he begins to lay the groundwork for keeping him around as his personal jester. Of course, Sir Pol has no inkling that this is the manner in which he is now being employed. He fancies himself Peregrine's tutor, but such a misapprehension of the situation is to be expected from an aspiring politician who visits foreign lands only to satisfy the whims of his domineering wife.

Act II, scene ii

1–27 This simple beat, which has as its backdrop Mosca and Nano setting the stage for Volpone's ensuing performance (yet another metatheatrical device: a stage within a stage), furthers the development of Sir Pol as a first-class idiot. His excitement over the impending arrival of a mountebank is near childlike and strangely endearing; however, his opinion of mountebanks is a direct inversion of their very nature. Mountebanks are quacks who exploit the sick and vulnerable by masquerading as professionals, but Sir Pol sees them as repositories of wisdom, be it medical or political. Sir Pol, though, is not the only individual in the play who mistakes a thing for its opposite. In fact, nearly every character in *Volpone* at some point confuses another character with his/her antipode: the legacy hunters believe the con artist Volpone is an invalid ripe for conning, Corvino is convinced that his chaste wife is the foulest slut in Venice and Lady Would-be mistakes the young man Peregrine for a woman. Thus, Sir Pol may be an undeniable moron, but is his folly any different from the folly of the other characters?

28–196 Of all the scenes featuring Volpone, this scene is typically considered to be the most overwritten and is usually trimmed in production. For nearly 170 lines, Volpone discourses on medicine and the charlatans who bastardize it, and he tries furiously to extract a mere six crowns from gullible audience members. The long lists and jargon involved in the former quickly grow tiresome while the comparative smallness of the latter appears pathetic and desperate. What is Volpone trying to achieve by this charade? This is the question that must trouble any actor playing Volpone. An actor needs to know his character's objective at all times, but Volpone's aim is ambiguous. Is his primary objective to get those in the crowd to give him money? If so, this shows that it is the financial manipulation of others, not the size of the gift, that brings Volpone joy. In other words, Volpone is not concerned with how much people give but with whether he has the power to make them hand over their money. There is a second way of seeing Volpone in this scene. Perhaps he is simply there to perform. Volpone has shown himself to be an actor who is addicted to the rush of performing before an audience. It is reasonable to believe that he wants nothing more than what every actor wants: to hold a group of people captive while he performs for them. When we leave Volpone in I.v, he is pondering a way to win Celia. After much or little contemplation, Volpone must have hatched the idea that he should disguise himself as the famous mountebank Scoto of Mantua and peddle elixirs under Celia's window. Why he thinks this particular disguise would forward his quest is never explored, nor should it be. It is, for all intents and purposes, irrelevant to Volpone's pursuit of Celia. At most his disguise provides a pretext for getting a glimpse of her face. In this reading Volpone pretends to be Scoto of Mantua not because the disguise aids him in winning Celia but because he has always wanted to play Scoto of Mantua and Celia serves as a convenient excuse. Of course, it is also possible that Volpone really is there for Celia. This view leads to a third reading of the scene. In this interpretation Volpone's sole objective is to get Celia to reveal herself. His antics are not done to amuse or engage the crowd but to draw Celia out of hiding. Such a Volpone would sneak furtive glances at Celia's window and grow more desperate and anxious as she fails to appear. His voice would grow louder and his behavior more frenzied in his attempt to get a glimpse of the woman locked in by her husband. This last interpretation is especially useful for an actor because it gives Volpone a clear obstacle to play against throughout the scene.

As for Volpone's disguise, what is its significance? Why would he choose (or Jonson choose for him) the guise of a mountebank? It is worth noting that the second incarnation of Volpone is an inversion of his persona in the first act. Volpone begins the play disguised as a false invalid promising riches to the healthy while in the second act he appears as a healer bringing a fraudulent cure to those frightened by the prospect of disease and aging. In both acts he preys on people's fear of death and dying. Volpone recognizes that the legacy hunters are displacing their fear of death. By anticipating Volpone's death, each denies the reality of his own death. Volpone's sickness is proof of their health. The less like him they look, the more alive the legacy hunters feel. This is especially true of Corbaccio. In contrast to the legacy hunters, the crowd is very much in touch with the reality of their eventual deaths, and Volpone attempts to exploit this awareness for profit. Thus, both of Volpone's disguises, the invalid and the false healer, help him tap into people's feelings of vulnerability and frailty.

197 to the end This is the moment when Celia appears, and her appearance changes the dynamic of the entire scene. Of course, this does not have to be the moment when Celia appears. Although Jonson's text indicates that Celia makes her appearance at this moment, stage directions in the modern theater are more suggestive than they are prescriptive; therefore, it is useful to consider other places in the scene where Celia might appear. What might the scene look like if her entrance coincides with Volpone's entrance at line 28? Similarly, how would the dynamic of the scene change if she does not appear until line 222 when Volpone requests the handkerchief? Whatever one decides, it is clear that Celia's entrance has a profound effect on Volpone. In subsequent scenes he details his immediate and intense infatuation with her, so one must account for how that sudden enchantment manifests itself in Volpone's behavior. It is possible that it causes him to break character and that Scoto of Mantua briefly or periodically turns into lovesick Volpone whenever he catches sight of Celia. It is also possible that he plays it off and intentionally avoids eye contact with the woman who has such a powerful effect on him although this choice seems to internalize the conflict and diminish the comic potential of Volpone alternating between doctor and paramour. One also must account for Celia's behavior during this scene. Is there anything in her attitude or movements that suggests she is flirting with Volpone, or is she merely an innocent victim of a lascivious male gaze? The key gesture is the dropping of the handkerchief. In the 17th century, there was nothing suggestive about the practice of dropping money in a handkerchief; however, the actress portraying Celia can choose to insert some innuendo into the exchange. Doing so would make Corvino appear slightly less paranoid and complicate the character of Celia, who on the surface appears to be a one-dimensional figure consumed with defending her virtue at all costs. Although undeniably more interesting and complex than the chaste

Celia, it is difficult to find the language in Jonson's text to support such a reading of the character. Thus, any production that goes this route may find itself at odds with the script.

Act II, scene iii

1 to the end   Despite its brevity, this crisp and chaotic scene is a turning point in the act. Corvino's arrival throws Volpone's unspecified plot into disarray. Beaten into a hasty retreat by the enraged and humiliated Corvino, Volpone is forced to abandon whatever plans he has for Celia. However, the winner in this situation is not Corvino but Mosca, for Volpone now once again requires the assistance of his trusty parasite to get him out of a jam. Consequently, the agency in the subsequent scenes of Act II moves from Volpone to Mosca. Corvino, although he does not realize it, makes his shame worse through his own actions. The irony of Corvino's outburst is that it draws attention to the very thing he wishes to keep hidden: his cuckolding. In all likelihood Celia's dropping of the handkerchief and any accompanying innuendo go unnoticed by the crowd, but Corvino undoubtedly makes them aware of it when he christens himself '*Pantalone di Besogniosi*'. As happens elsewhere in the play, Corvino brings about his worst fear in a misguided attempt to avoid it. In addition to being pregnant with irony, Corvino's attack on Volpone/Scoto is full of opportunities for physical comedy. Any director must consider the following questions: How and with what does Corvino attack Volpone? Is Corvino a skilled fighter or an amateur posing as a ringer? What happens to Volpone during the confrontation? Does he lose part of his disguise in the melee? Does he shriek and run around like a drama queen? What is the crowd's point of view? Are they egging Corvino on because they are eager for a fight, or are they simply trying to escape a volatile situation? Like most fight scenes, the challenge of this scene is to embrace its chaos while still delineating each character's action. It is not an easy thing to do, but if it is done well and the choices are creative, then an audience can find the scuffle quite amusing.

Act II, scene iv

1 to the end   After being vanquished in the skirmish, Volpone returns with Mosca to regroup and strategize. Although there are subtle hints of his vulnerability and neediness in Act I, this is the first time in the play that Volpone's emotional frailty is on full display. The events of the preceding scenes have left him shaken. Celia has struck his heart, and Corvino has struck his body. He feels the former more than the latter, and the intensity of his ardor leads him to make a series of hasty, ill-conceived decisions in the ensuing scenes. The first of these decisions occurs here on lines 21–3. He gives Mosca the keys to his fortune (a choice that he will repeat in Act V), thereby surrendering all power to his parasite. Volpone may still retain the title of master, but it is abundantly clear that Mosca is now the one calling the shots. The impetuousness of Volpone is in stark contrast to the deliberateness of Mosca. Volpone has spent years amassing his fortune and orchestrating this con, yet in an instant he forfeits it all for a shot at a married woman. There is no evidence that he has weighed the costs and benefits of this course of action. He simply wants what he wants, and he is willing to surrender everything to satisfy a fleeting desire. Volpone's need for immediate gratification resembles that of a bratty child, and it undoes him again and again. One could even argue that it is his tragic flaw. Another of Volpone's weaknesses is also on display in this scene: his incessant need for approval and reassurance. Volpone suffers from acute insecurity. At the end of this scene, he looks to Mosca for reassurance. He desperately wants to hear that his performance as Scoto of Mantua was convincing. In this way Volpone is like so many actors who crave approval yet secretly doubt their talent. More than anything else, Volpone is a performer in need of applause; and this scene, maybe more than any other in the play, demonstrates that. Thus, Jonson in II.iv is advancing the plot while simultaneously filling in the portrait of Volpone that he merely hints at in Act I. Only occasionally do we get to see Volpone not playing a character; so when it happens, as it does here, we must give the scene our full attention. Otherwise, we run the risk of missing out on all of Volpone's complexities.

Act II, scene v

1–28   Along with II.vii and III.vii, this scene raises serious questions about the tone of the play. Just as the freaks present a challenge for a director seeking a unified aesthetic, Corvino's (and later Volpone's) abuse of Celia makes it difficult to find a consistent and appropriate tone for a production. After all, *Volpone* is a comedy, and the action up until this point has been humorous. The same can be said for much of the action in the ensuing acts; however, there is something undeniably disquieting about bearing witness to violence against women. When first produced in 1606, *Volpone* did not present such a problem. Celia was portrayed by a young boy, and threats of domestic violence were hardly considered criminal behavior. The passage of time has changed all that, and the gap between Jacobean mores and contemporary values has made these scenes quite problematic for modern directors. Of course, it is possible to treat this interaction glibly and perform it like a couple's squabble in *Commedia dell'Arte*. Such an approach, though, ignores the dark underbelly of Jonson's comedy and runs the risk of offending a modern audience with its superficial treatment of domestic violence. Ultimately, to be successful a production cannot shy away from the bleak elements in *Volpone*, but it cannot become so fixated on them that an audience feels they no longer have permission to laugh at the humorous aspects of the play. How one strikes this balance is a conundrum that continues to confound modern directors. Perhaps it is inevitable that contemporary productions of *Volpone* will be tonally schizophrenic; nevertheless, one cannot stop searching for a thread that unites all the disparate elements of this cynical, playful, bizarre and menacing comedy.

In this 73-line scene, only seven lines belong to Celia. Corvino's rage is overwhelming, especially when directed at someone as timid as Celia. Celia also knows better than to challenge her husband when he is so agitated. Consequently, she lets him hurl uninterrupted vituperations for the first 28 lines of the scene. What, though, are we to make of Corvino's outburst? Is it merely bluster that Celia has learned to humor over the course of their marriage, or is this situation dangerously different from the outset? In addition, what is it that has incensed Corvino so much? As an audience, we already know that Corvino is notoriously jealous of other men and exceptionally suspicious of his wife. We also know that he is motivated by a powerful fear of public humiliation. For Corvino no shame is greater than having his wife publicly flirt with another man, thereby alluding to his inadequacy as a lover and a man. These factors all converge to engender a response in Corvino that is wildly disproportionate to Celia's offense (if Celia even did anything wrong). As happens in nearly every abusive relationship (and the relationship between Corvino and Celia is a textbook case of domestic violence), Corvino behaves violently toward Celia because he wants to exert power over her. He does not want to hurt her so much as he wants to control her. Similar to many men in both Jacobean times and modern society, Corvino believes that his wife belongs to him and that he can do with her as he wishes. When she behaves in a way that he finds inappropriate, he uses fear and intimidation to manipulate her. Ultimately, there is nothing that Celia can do to appease Corvino because what he seeks is limitless power. Even if Celia never made a mistake, Corvino would invent mistakes so that he would have a pretext for augmenting his power. That is what abusers do.

Despite Corvino's extreme possessiveness, he has some rather peculiar fantasies involving Celia and other men. In lines 15–20, Corvino envisions the mountebank massaging Celia's genitals before Celia mounts him in coitus. As troubled as Corvino is by the thought, he also seems oddly titillated by it. It is a classic example of a person's deepest fear also being his deepest yearning. Perhaps this fantasy explains Corvino's willingness in the following scene to offer his wife up to Volpone since it is something that he has already fantasized unwittingly about. Thus, Corvino, the man so covetous of his wife, subtly reveals in this scene and the next scene that he is aroused by the idea of Celia sleeping with other men. The Jonsonian irony could not be more apparent.

29 to the end Rather than soothing Corvino, Celia's plea for patience at line 29 only causes the situation to escalate. Corvino, who up until this point has only verbally threatened his wife, now begins brandishing a knife and threatening physical violence. The stakes have risen, and the limits of Corvino's anger are unknown. The scene immediately becomes fraught with suspense as the audience tries to guess how far this madman will go. Celia, too, seems surprised by the extreme nature of Corvino's response. Clearly, there is something about this altercation that is different and more intense than the unhappy couple's prior conflicts. That is what makes this scene so riveting. A skilled dramatist knows that s/he must present the most dangerous and unique moments in his/her characters' lives while discarding those moments of secondary importance. More than anything else, playwriting comes down to scene selection, and Jonson shows here that he knows what to put on the stage and what to keep off of it.

As the scene unfolds, we learn two very important things about Corvino: he thinks all life is a performance, and he is a sexual sadist. In lines 3–9 of the scene, Corvino claims that the mountebank's audience, like spectators, lecherously watched Celia; and then in line 40 he refers to Celia as an actor. As a perpetual con man and liar, Corvino cannot fathom the existence of honest people who are what they appear to be. Because his entire life is a carefully constructed performance, he presumes that everyone else, including his wife, is also performing. What makes Celia and Bonario unique in the landscape of the play is that they are not performers. They are individuals capable of authenticity, and it is this trait that makes them suspect and social outcasts. (It is also what makes them frequently come across as bland and uninspired in production, for how can their purity compare to Volpone's antics, Mosca's brilliance or the legacy hunters' eccentricities? Furthermore, their refusal to join the other characters' games, while laudable, causes Celia and Bonario to appear humorless and joyless, hardly virtues in a comedy.) In a society where lies are mistaken for truths and truths are mistaken for lies, it is the honest men and women who suffer. Thus, Celia's virtue becomes vice in a Venice where everything is confused with its opposite, and it is performance which is at the root of all this confusion.

Following this extended theatrical metaphor, Corvino changes course and concludes the scene by enumerating a lengthy list of punishments he plans to inflict upon Celia. These punishments include bondage, a chastity belt, repeated anal sex and public dissection. Thus, by the end of the scene, Jonson has established Corvino as someone whose sexual fetishes place him far outside the mainstream of society. An awareness of these fetishes can prove especially useful for set and costume designers as they think about the interior of Corvino's house and the clothing that he and his wife might wear.

Act II, scene vi

1–31 In Mosca's previous scene, he vows to assist Volpone in his attempt to win Celia and cuckold Corvino; however, he never discloses his plans, which means that the audience is in the dark about where this scene between Mosca and Corvino might be heading. In marked contrast to Shakespeare's characters, who almost always publicly declare their strategy before embarking on a course of action, Jonson's characters, especially the masterful tricksters like Mosca, frequently hold their cards close to their vests. Shakespeare's plays are rife with dramatic irony while Jonson's plays often leave the audience as clueless as the other characters are. Thus, Shakespeare's plays afford the audience the pleasure of being in on a secret while Jonson's plays allow the public to be surprised. Another difference is that Shakespeare's approach allows the audience to feel intelligent and special while Jonson's approach, which befits his elitist disposition, reminds audience members of their ignorance. This is why Mosca's announcement that Volpone has been cured by Scoto's oil catches everyone, Corvino and audience alike, by surprise. We are taking in this information at the same time that the character is processing it. Unlike Corvino, we have the added benefit of knowing that Mosca is lying; nevertheless, the nature of the lie still comes as a surprise. This lie is also the perfect thing to tell Corvino. Not only does it incense him, but it also undermines all of the assumptions that he has made about Scoto. This, in turn, causes Corvino to question the very nature of his judgment. No longer believing that he can distinguish between what is truthful and what is fraudulent, Corvino becomes more likely to delegate his decision making to Mosca. Having thrown Corvino off balance, Mosca can now go in for the kill.

31 to the end The first 30 lines of this scene are merely a prologue to what Mosca begins midway through line 31. By announcing that Volpone can only be cured if he sleeps next to a lusty and juicy woman, Mosca leaves the setup behind and gets to the heart of the matter: his suggestion that Corvino agree to let his wife sleep in the same bed with Volpone. Like all of Mosca's suggestions in the play, this suggestion is subliminal. Mosca recognizes that the men around him need to feel powerful and in control, so he subtly hints at things, thereby allowing others to believe that they are the ones who have originated the idea. Corvino, however, is not as quick on the uptake as Mosca would like. Hence, Mosca's excessive and comic repetition of 'think' at line 59. Unable to coax out the answer he desires from Corvino, Mosca adopts a new and more successful tactic beginning at line 60: he exploits Corvino's jealousy and competitiveness. By making Corvino think that some fictitious doctor has outdone him,

Mosca hits Corvino in his weak spot; and within a matter of lines, Corvino has caved and is offering up his wife to Volpone. It is worth noting that right before Corvino takes the plunge he alludes to the investment he has already made in pursuit of Volpone's fortune. Like Corbaccio in I.iv, Corvino feels that he has too much at stake to walk away from the table just yet. Consequently, he makes a foolish gamble and adds his wife to the pot, where she joins Corbaccio's son. And so Corvino, like Corbaccio before him, dissolves a sacred familial relationship in his foolhardy attempt to strike it rich, and Mosca again proves that there is nothing he cannot get a man to sacrifice if the circumstances are right.

Act II, scene vii

1 to the end This 18-line scene between Corvino and Celia is disarmingly simple. At first glance it looks like nothing more than a disingenuous attempt by Corvino to lure Celia into the ambush awaiting her at Volpone's house. It is tempting to have Corvino play it with sarcasm and for Celia to respond with incredulity, but such an approach ignores the possibility of complexity within their relationship. Is it so farfetched to think that Corvino can believably feign contrition, and is it unreasonable to assume that Celia might be duped by such an act? The stage directions indicate that Celia kisses him at line 13, yet we do not know how or why she kisses him. Perhaps it is because she is afraid to disobey his command; however, it is equally plausible that she assumes Corvino is reformed and repentant. In 1979 psychologist Lenore Walker famously asserted that all abusive relationships follow a predictable pattern: tensions build between the couple, a crisis erupts, an abusive event takes place, the abuser expresses remorse and the couple reconciles until the cycle begins again. The only thing that can break this pattern of behavior is if the victim terminates the relationship. If one applies Walker's model to the relationship between Corvino and Celia, then it immediately becomes apparent why Celia might take Corvino at his word in this scene. If the couple is cycling, then it makes sense for Celia to conclude that the crisis has passed and that they are now entering the next phase of the cycle. What Celia does not know is that Corvino has merely devised a new way to batter her: whore her out to another man.

Act III

Act III, scene i

1 to the end There are several places where it would be logical to place an intermission, but arguably the most appropriate location is between Act II and Act III. Although dividing a production in this way would undoubtedly make the second act run noticeably longer than the first, it does give the production a nice symmetry since the first act begins with a long speech by Volpone while this act opens with a fitting counterpoint spoken by Mosca. The play's symmetry becomes even more apparent in print if one examines the opening scene in each of the five acts. Act I and Act V begin with a speech by Volpone, Act II and Act IV start with a scene between Sir Pol and Peregrine and Act III commences with a speech by Mosca. The play is a perfectly balanced seesaw with Mosca situated in the middle like a fulcrum or pivot point upon which the other characters' fortunes travel upward and downward.

Mosca's speech at the top of the third act is also distinct in the landscape of the play because it is the first of two times (the other occurring in V.v) that the closely guarded parasite gives the public a glimpse into the inner workings of his mind, and what the audience sees is none too flattering. Mosca exposes himself as a narcissist who is convinced that his accomplishments endow him with a special status on earth. He conceives of himself as an artist, and he espouses a harrowing worldview – perhaps one that is shared by Jonson – that 'all the wise world is little else in nature but parasites or sub-parasites'. This pointed commentary should jolt audience members out of their complacency and bring them to a realization that they are no different from the bestial con men populating the stage. In addition, this speech reveals much about Mosca's physical type and manner of motion. He compares himself to a snake, labels himself limber and nimble and trumpets his ability to be 'there, and here, and yonder, all at once'. These descriptions all point to an individual who is lean, agile and stealthy. They also characterize someone who can be anywhere and can become anyone at a moment's notice. In contrast to Volpone, who relies extensively on costumes and other adornments to enter into character, Mosca shows himself to be a true chameleon who can get by on only his ingenuity and talent. In other words, Volpone is the kind of performer who announces to the world that he is acting while Mosca is so subtle that one forgets a performance is even taking place. Without this speech that distinction between the two men might go unnoticed.

Act III, scene ii

1–35 After boasting of his prowess as a performer, Mosca shows the audience exactly what he is capable of. This scene can be divided into two parts. In the first half of the scene, Mosca merely wants to establish his credibility with Bonario, the one character who does not immediately trust him. Remarkably, all it takes is a few well-timed tears and an impassioned speech in which Mosca admits that he is overly sycophantic toward his master while denying that he is dishonest or corrupt. (Note the irony here. This is the exact moment in the play that Mosca stops following Volpone's orders and begins to do more than his master has empowered him to do.) Bonario's rapid change of heart is certainly a testament to Mosca's skill; however, it is also an indicator of Bonario's density. Like Celia, Bonario comes across as colorless and largely ineffectual. This scene, which introduces him to the audience, hardly establishes him as a hero worthy of our support. If we were holding out hope for a noble character who could match Mosca and Volpone blow for blow, then Jonson swiftly and soundly dismisses those aspirations at the beginning of this scene. Bonario, the dullard, is not going to take down Mosca and Volpone. If Mosca and Volpone fall, then it will be by their own hands. In Jonson's world good does not defeat evil. Evil, if it loses at all, defeats itself.

36 to the end Having won Bonario's trust, Mosca can now pursue his more sinister goal of setting a son against a disloyal father. While Mosca's objective is clear in this moment, his motivation is ambiguous. What does Mosca hope to accomplish by divulging this information? Does he simply want to unleash more hurt and chaos? Does he think that Bonario will become so enraged that he will unthinkingly commit patricide? Is this part of his larger plot against Volpone, or has that plot not begun to take shape yet? Even if this is not part of Mosca's plan to unseat Volpone, it is undeniably the beginning of Mosca's insurrection. He is deviating from Volpone's script and doing things behind his master's back. He is inviting a stranger into the house and sharing precious secrets with him. It is a dangerous game he is playing with no discernible financial benefit, so why does he do it? One possible answer is that Mosca, like Volpone, is a thrill seeker. The high of tricking Corvino has already worn off, and he must move on to his next conquest and victim. By modern criminal standards, Mosca is a psychopath. He is an individual devoid of empathy. He shows no remorse for his actions and is incapable of ceasing his destructive behavior. As every criminologist knows, psychopaths almost always engage in increasingly risky behavior. Each crime must be more difficult and inflict a greater amount of suffering than the previous crime. The psychopath must constantly outdo himself or he feels unfulfilled. Intervals between crimes shrink as the temporary high generated by the 'achievement' becomes less and less satisfying. Interestingly, audience members also seem to derive an increasing amount of pleasure from Mosca's misdeeds. Like Mosca, they wish to see the limits of the parasite's power. Thus, while Mosca is undeniably an antihero, his villainy appeals to viewers who live vicariously through him even as they root for his downfall. Seen from the perspective of modern psychology and criminology, Mosca's behavior as well as the audience's response to his actions become more understandable.

Act III, scene iii

1 to the end While Mosca is out playing, Volpone is at home anxiously waiting and warding off boredom. Unbeknownst to Volpone, his servant has tarried and gone off in search of additional adventure. Mosca's detour leaves Volpone in limbo. We already know that Volpone craves immediate gratification and that his lust for Celia is strong, so it is logical to conclude that Mosca's tardiness has made Volpone more than a little edgy. His fate is in Mosca's hands, and he can do nothing but pass the time until Mosca returns with news. Thus, the juxtaposition of this scene and the previous scene serves as a potent reminder of Volpone's impotence when his parasite is absent. By outsourcing his hopes to Mosca, he has relegated himself to spectator status in the play that bears his name. Fittingly, Volpone makes himself a spectator to another show while he awaits Mosca's return. Like I.ii, this metatheatrical scene features a performance within a performance: the three freaks act out an argument over who should be most beloved by Volpone. As Brian Parker points out in his footnote, this debate parallels the struggle occurring between the three legacy hunters. In fact, it can be thought of as a burlesque of the play's central plotline. It reveals the triviality of such contests, and it allows the audience to see the legacy hunters for the freaks they really are. In doing so, it calls to mind one of Dr. Astrov's lines in Anton Chekhov's *Uncle Vanya*: 'I used to think freaks were sick, but I've changed my mind. Now I think being a freak is the normal human condition.' It is hard not to wonder if this is Ben Jonson's view of the world as well. Much to Volpone's chagrin, the freaks' burlesque is interrupted by the arrival of another grotesque individual: the oft talked about Lady Would-be. And so, as this scene transitions into the next, Volpone moves from a willing audience member to an unwilling audience member held captive by an amateur actress who has forced her way onto the stage. Volpone's progression from empowered actor to disempowered spectator is now complete.

Act III, scene iv

1–38 Although much is said about the irrepressible Lady Would-be in the first two acts, she does not appear until Act III. If the production has done its job, Lady Would-be should be an even more revolting monstrosity than the audience has imagined. She should look like Volpone's worst nightmare, a woman so hideous and vile that she is capable of turning his penis permanently flaccid. As she swiftly removes her collar to reveal an excessive portion of her fatty breast, the audience should squirm in discomfort just as Volpone does. Lady Would-be is truly a terror. With the intelligence of a cow, the chattiness of a parrot and the temperament of a tornado, she dominates the room with her diminutive intellect. Jonson, however, does something very crafty when he introduces this beast masquerading as a woman of a culture. He does not immediately sic her on Volpone; instead, he has her chew out her innocent serving ladies first while Volpone and Nano watch with horror and dread. This prelude to the real fireworks is the perfect beginning to the scene. It establishes Lady Would-be as a force to be reckoned with, and it whets the audience's appetite for the terrible confrontation to come. Like Volpone, we can see the storm coming, but unlike Volpone, we eagerly anticipate the thunder, lightning and destruction.

39 to the end   The scene between Volpone and Lady Would-be is one of the play's funniest. It is yet another example of Volpone being trapped by his feigned infirmity. Only this time Mosca is not around to rescue him. A prisoner in his own bed, Volpone has no choice but to suffer through Lady Would-be's prattling. And prattle she does. Nearly half of Lady Would-be's lines in this scene take the form of a list. She enumerates everything from holistic remedies to poets. Much like a list song in musical theater, the endless catalogues of Lady Would-be become more humorous as the items proliferate. Lady Would-be also shows herself to be a worthy partner for her dimwitted husband. She is every bit as stupid, uttering malapropisms indiscriminately. But the scene is about more than Lady Would-be's inane chatter. It is about what she is doing to Volpone while she runs her mouth. For this scene to succeed, the comedy must be as physical as it is verbal. The great acting guru Sandy Meisner spoke extensively about 'the pinch and the ouch' on stage. In Meisner's theory, 'the ouch' of one character must be directly proportional to 'the pinch' that s/he receives from another character. In III.iv, we see a very loud and passionate 'ouch' from Volpone that culminates in a series of punctuated exclamations in his final lines of the scene. (Note the difference between the punctuation of Volpone's early lines in the scene and the punctuation of his concluding lines. The change in punctuation suggests that Volpone's exasperation builds to a crescendo. It is essential that the actor playing Volpone not begin the scene too upset. If he does, then the scene will become repetitive because the actor playing Volpone has left himself no place to go.) What has Lady Would-be done to make Volpone passionately cry out for salvation? Surely her offense must be greater than an overactive mouth. We know from her excessive cleavage that she is plotting a seduction. Her language also becomes more sexual as the scene progresses. (See 'passions' at line 101, the double entendre 'politic bodies' at line 104 and 'lusty' at line 114.) All of this indicates that she pursues greater physical intimacy with Volpone as the scene moves toward its climax. When she compares Volpone to a former lover who would sleep while she discoursed, it is hard not to imagine her crawling into bed with the hapless Volpone, smothering him with kisses and cradling him in her bear-sized arms. Of course, this is Jonsonian poetic justice since Volpone's healing requires a woman who is 'lusty and full of juice to sleep by him'.

Act III, scene v

1–29 Fortunately for Volpone, his 'good angel' Mosca arrives in time to redeem him before Lady Would-be can have her way with his body. As always, Mosca handles the situation efficiently. It is almost as if he comes armed with a lie for every situation. In this instance, he dispatches Lady Would-be by insinuating that Sir Pol is presently cheating on her with a younger woman. The irony of the faithless Lady Would-be suspecting the faithful Sir Pol of infidelity is both amusing and profound, for as Mosca observes, it is cheaters who are most prone to fits of jealousy. This scene also builds on the comedy of the previous scene, culminating in a false exit and a bizarre request. When Lady Would-be returns at line 26, we delight in the resumption of Volpone's misfortune (an exercise in *schadenfreude*) and are amused that in her haste Lady Would-be neglected to ask the location of her husband. Before departing a second time, Lady Would-be delivers one of the play's funniest lines: 'I pray you, lend me your dwarf.' The request is completely inexplicable, and one feels more than a tinge of sympathy for the poor dwarf drafted against his will into an army captained by a bumbling monster. Although Jonson does not have Nano on stage for this moment, it might be worthwhile to bring him (and possibly Castrone and Androgyno) back out when Mosca enters so that we get the comic payoff of seeing his response to Lady Would-be's request.

30 to the end With Lady Would-be dispatched, Volpone can go back to his designs and the play can resume its central story. In these economical eight lines, Mosca tempts Volpone with thoughts of carnal success and prepares him for the arrival of Corbaccio. His vigor returned to him, Volpone is again like a gambler eagerly awaiting the next hand. As an audience, we can sense that the comic British interlude is over and the Venetian intrigue is about to resume. How it will play out, though, is still very much in doubt. Thus, this cliffhanger, neatly encapsulated by Volpone's 'I lie, and draw – for an encounter', makes the conclusion of this scene another common location for an intermission.

Act III, scene vi

1 to the end The shortest scene in the play is one of its most pivotal. When he invites Bonario into the house and gives him a view of the game being played by Volpone and others, Mosca unwittingly sows the seeds of catastrophe. This scene is ultimately about concealment and revelation. Bonario's presence is hidden from Volpone and the legacy hunters, and it is this concealment that gives him a window into their secret lives. The paradox of the situation is neatly encapsulated in Mosca's opening line: 'Here concealed, you may hear all.' Thus, Mosca's shrouding of Bonario ensures that every last deception will eventually be revealed by the play's end.

Act III, scene vii

1–18 Although Mosca encountered unexpected arrivals and unpleasant situations earlier in the play, this is the first moment when something goes discernibly wrong. After instructing Corvino to refrain from coming immediately, Mosca is quite surprised when Corvino's arrival precedes Corbaccio's. As a playwright, Mosca has lost control of his characters for the first time. They are no longer entering and exiting on their assigned cues. This loss of control should cause him a certain amount of anxiety as he handles his first full-blown crisis. Mosca, as always, works quickly; and by the end of this beat, it seems as if he has solved the problem by sequestering Bonario in a remote corner of the house. Nevertheless, there is probably a lingering worry in Mosca's mind, despite his seeming confidence in lines 17–8, that the danger represented by Bonario has not passed. Perhaps this concern manifests itself in Mosca's behavior in the ensuing beats. Certainly the audience can sense the storm brewing. When Bonario admits at line 16 that his distrust of Mosca has returned, it is a clue to the audience that this problem will not be solved as easily as the ones before it.

19–67 When compared to the beat that follows it, this exchange between Corvino and Celia is cordial if not downright pleasant. Corvino does not immediately berate his wife. Rather he starts with reason and tries to coax her over to his position. He explains the financial ramifications of the situation, promises confidentiality and rebuts her moral concerns. As indicated by lines 20–3, he is firm but has not yet lost his temper. Two things are striking about Corvino's request. The first is his dismissal of the importance of honor. It is a complete reversal of his concern in II.v, which centers entirely on honor and shame. (That scene begins with Corvino exclaiming, 'Death of mine honor'.) A closer examination of this scene, however, shows that Corvino has not forgotten about honor but has simply redefined it. Previously, Corvino linked honor with fidelity. In his mind any sign that a wife is cheating brings shame upon the husband. Here he discards that definition and instead links honor with obedience in lines 30–1. According to Corvino's new view, a husband is dishonored when his wife disobeys him even if he is commanding her to be unfaithful. A man's masculinity is now called into question if he cannot bend a woman to his every whim. Eventually, when Celia continues to challenge him in front of Mosca and Volpone, Corvino will erupt in anger because he believes a woman has no right to publicly undermine his power and rights as a man. The second thing that is startling about Corvino's request is his assertion that Celia's lying in bed with another man is a virtuous act. Perhaps this is simply a tactic designed to win Celia over, but it is also quite plausible that he believes what he is saying. In Corvino's mind immorality has become piety while piety has become immorality. It is yet another example of inversion in the upside-down world that Jonson has created.

68–132 The inverted value system depicted in *Volpone* is mirrored in the play's structure. Just as Volpone's disguise as Scoto inverts his disguise as the invalid, this beat is a reversal of II.v. Corvino again threatens Celia with disfigurement and public humiliation; however, he makes the threat for the opposite reason. Previously he vowed to torture her because he thought she was flirting with Scoto (Volpone in actuality), and now he promises to inflict a similar punishment if she does not climb into bed with Volpone. The inversion is too perfect to be merely coincidental or even just another example of Jonsonian irony: it is powerful evidence of the carefully constructed marriage between form and content in the play.

As for what this beat reveals about the personalities of Corvino and Celia, there are several things worth noting. Once more, Corvino outs himself as a sadist, but what is so jarring in this exchange is the speed at which he alternates between torturer and charmer. Like all abusers, Corvino will do or say anything to establish control over his victim. One moment he terrorizes, and the next he behaves tenderly. (Note the saccharine address of 'sweet Celia' as he departs.) Both his threats and bribes are equally powerful forms of emotional manipulation even though neither tactic helps Corvino assert dominance over Celia in this instance. Celia, however, is not merely a bystander to Corvino's cruelty. A cursory reading might give one the sense that she is simply someone who will do anything to preserve her honor, and while this interpretation is not inaccurate, it is also not complete. Celia is all too willing to suffer the punishments devised by Corvino, and she is alarmingly overeager when she volunteers to swallow poison or eat coals. It is almost as if she yearns to be a martyr. Thus, it is reasonable to wonder if Jonson is suggesting that Celia is motivated by more than piety and that she derives some perverse pleasure from pain. These masochistic tendencies, which are hinted at in this beat, will become even more apparent in the beats that follow.

133–238 This beat, too, is an inversion of a prior scene. It reverses the situation of III.iv. In that scene the aggressive and talkative Lady Would-be holds Volpone captive while in this scene Volpone is the captor and Celia the victim of his unwanted advances. Although not ridden with the malapropisms that plague Lady Would-be's speech, Volpone's language is equally florid. Like Lady Would-be, Volpone communicates using a series of seemingly endless lists that catalogue everything from jewelry and birds to the roles he imagines playing with Celia. In a play about uncontrolled consumption, these lists embody the unchecked appetites of the characters. They testify to their belief that more is always better. Their language is excessive because their lives are full of excess. One victim of these unchecked appetites is Celia, whose request to be blasted or struck by lightning bears a striking resemblance to Volpone's pleas in III.iv. Thus, the similarities between the two scenes are yet another reminder that these characters inhabit a world that is perpetually flipping on its axis.

This beat is significant for another reason: it presents us with the third incarnation of Volpone. After portraying the invalid and the mountebank, he now takes on the persona of the dashing young lover who tries to leap, sing and talk his way into a lady's heart and body. This kinetic, invigorated Volpone who bounds out of bed is not something that we have previously seen, for up until this moment he has been crippled by his primary disguise as a dying man. This new incarnation should surprise the audience with its vivacity and ardor. In short, Volpone is speaking as much to Celia as he is to the audience when he asks, 'Why art thou mazed to see me thus revived?' Volpone also sees this moment as a reprisal of a role he once performed for Venetian dignitaries. He is using Celia to relive past stage glories. It is as if he has lost the ability to distinguish between the world of life and the world of theater. For Volpone life in its ideal state is nothing more than a ceaseless series of performances. He lays out this idealized vision of existence in lines 218–38. It should be noted that his fantasies of passing seamlessly from one role into the next mirror the freaks' commentary in I.ii on the transmigration of souls. This vision, though, is a nightmare for someone like Celia who craves authenticity in a fraudulent world.

239–65 The extent of Celia's frustration and horror becomes apparent in her speech that begins on line 239. Up until this moment, she seems to be in a state of disbelief and is nothing more than a stunned onlooker as Volpone makes a mockery of love; however, as the scene progresses, she slowly collects herself and by line 239 reaches a breaking point. She implores Volpone to show mercy by flaying her face or disfiguring her with leprosy. Needless to say, it is a strange and twisted concept of mercy. In fact, her request of Volpone is nearly identical to the earlier threats that Corvino directed at her. Of course, it is possible to interpret Celia's masochism as the martyrdom of a virtuous woman, but such an interpretation misses Jonson's critique of the overly devout. Upon further consideration, Celia's request appears more ridiculous than noble. Her piety, while perhaps commendable, is so extreme that one cannot help but question its usefulness in this situation. Is wrath, as Celia suggests, truly a lesser evil than lust? Even though Celia is undeniably a wronged woman, her overzealous guarding of her honor (particularly given the nature of her marriage) marks her as an extremist and distances her from a contemporary audience.

If Celia distances herself from the audience in this beat, then Volpone completely alienates himself from a viewing public that has up until this moment been somewhat favorably disposed toward him. This is the pivotal moment in the play because Volpone attacks an innocent for the first time. Before this incident, Volpone's antics are amusing and benign because they are directed at those who deserve to suffer. While far from decent, Volpone still appears likeable in comparison to his cruel servant and the avaricious legacy hunters, but this moment irrevocably changes that. Failing at persuasion, Volpone decides to take Celia by force. His brains and wit, cardinal virtues in Jonson's middle comedies, give way to brawn and might. This act, in addition to bringing yet more darkness to the play, transforms Volpone from a clever trickster to a brutal rapist. It is a decision that will define him in the eyes of the law and of the audience for the duration of the play.

266 to the end Despite Volpone's intent, his rape of Celia is unconsummated because the secluded Bonario emerges from hiding to play the semi-competent knight to Celia's damsel in distress. From where does Bonario appear, though? Has he slowly made his way back down to his initial hiding spot? Is this something that happens in view of the audience, thereby eliminating the element of surprise but increasing the dramatic irony? Or does he, as Jonson's stage direction suggests, leap out from the spot where Mosca has placed him? If so, does that mean Mosca grossly miscalculated what Bonario could and could not hear? Although the second option makes for an unanticipated entrance, it also raises legitimate questions about why the typically meticulous Mosca would choose such a poor location to conceal Bonario. Once on the stage, Bonario is moderately successful in his attempt to rescue Celia. He accomplishes his objective of prying her away from Volpone, but he makes the terrible mistake of leaving Volpone to the judicial system. Bonario places his trust in the law, and it is this misplaced trust in a corrupt institution that will bring Celia and him much hardship in the subsequent act.

Act III, scene viii

1 to the end For the first time in the play, Volpone and Mosca confront a crisis that appears too difficult to solve. All of their earlier bravado vanishes in this moment of intense vulnerability. Paradoxically, in the aftermath of Volpone's depraved sexual assault, his humanity finally emerges. He and Mosca appear as nothing more than two frightened individuals who believe that the hour of their punishment has arrived. Their mutual terror at the thought of branding and ear cropping is the first genuine emotion exhibited by either man. As Volpone observes at the conclusion of the previous scene, he is 'unmasked'. This unmasking refers to more than just the discovery of his con: it expresses a sentiment that the time for acting has passed and that his true self will at last be revealed to the world. That sentiment comes to a brief fruition in this scene.

Volpone's and Mosca's panic make this scene exceptionally frenetic. Almost every line is a shared line, which means Mosca and Volpone are cutting each other off at every possible opportunity. In addition, Mosca is in physical distress, having suffered a wound to the face at Bonario's hand. (There is a fitting justice in this since earlier Mosca agreed to let Bonario strike him across the face with a sword should he prove dishonest.) When Volpone hears someone coming and assumes that it is an officer of the law, the characters' terror intensifies. As Mosca goes to open the door, it appears that the chickens have finally come home to roost for the two con artists. Everyone, characters and audience alike, is bracing for an arrest; so when the door opens to reveal the crusty and forgotten Corbaccio, it is quite the amusing curveball.

Act III, scene ix

1–15 Does Mosca treat Corbaccio's arrival as a nuisance and distraction in a tumultuous time, or does he immediately recognize it as the lifeboat that he and Volpone need? Although either interpretation is workable, it seems that the latter is more grounded in the text. During this short exchange, Mosca returns to his former self. He once again showcases his ability to invent any lie for any occasion. In contrast to the previous scene, which features an out of sorts Mosca uncharacteristically telling the truth, this scene presents Mosca doing what he does best: manipulating people with a litany of masterful fabrications. Corbaccio's entrance appears to restore Mosca, reminding him that he is made to handle crises such as these. When the door opens on someone other than an officer of the law, it is the reprieve that Mosca needs to regroup and plot his way out of the mess that Volpone and he now find themselves in.

15 to the end Although Voltore's arrival temporarily complicates the situation, it ultimately works to Mosca's advantage. A skilled lawyer, Voltore is an invaluable asset in Volpone and Mosca's quest for exoneration. Once Mosca convinces Voltore that he has not betrayed him, which happens at line 40, he is then in a position to enlist him in the cause. It takes little effort to win over Voltore, and soon Voltore is requesting the presence of Corvino. With Corvino's arrival imminent, it is clear that the legacy hunters all have a common interest: protecting Volpone. The lines have been drawn. Evil is allied with evil, and good is allied with good. No longer is *Volpone* merely a play about bad men playing a dangerous game by themselves. It is now a cosmic battle between virtue and vice. Jonson has orchestrated the events so that the final two acts will be a confrontation between the forces of darkness (Volpone, Mosca and the legacy hunters) and the forces of light (Bonario and Celia). Only one can prevail, and at this juncture it is unclear who will triumph in the trial.

Act IV

Act IV, scene i

1 to the end With the characters' fates in limbo and a full-blown crisis brewing, the audience is anxious to see how everything will play out; so it is the perfect time for another comic interlude featuring the bumbling English knight Sir Politic Would-be, right? Like the opening scene of Act II, this scene seems to materialize out of nowhere. Why would we possibly be concerned with the ramblings of a nincompoop when an attempted rape has just occurred and a trial is about to begin? What does this scene contribute to the play to merit its inclusion? Perhaps most importantly, this scene and the two scenes that follow it give the audience a sense that time has passed between the conclusion of Act III and the congregating of Mosca and the legacy hunters in IV.iv. In a play where time appears to move continuously from morning to night without any jumps forward, the opening of Act IV buys Jonson the time that he needs to get Mosca and the legacy hunters together in one location. (It should be noted, however, that the same effect could be achieved in contemporary productions by placing an intermission at the end of Act III and resuming the play at IV.iv.)

As for the content of this scene, it picks up where we last left Sir Pol and Peregrine. Sir Pol still fancies himself the young man's tutor, and Peregrine continues to use the knight as his personal jester. Even though it is one continuous conversation, this scene can be thought of as three parts: Sir Pol's description of Venetian mores, Sir Pol's declaration of his business plans and Peregrine's reading of Sir Pol's diary. Aside from the irony of Sir Pol instructing Peregrine to refrain from speaking to strangers, Sir Pol's description of Venetian life is uncharacteristically accurate and a useful guide for an English audience looking to enter the exotic and sinister Venetian world that Jonson has created. In particular, his admonition to 'never speak a truth' is quite resonant given all that has transpired and all that will transpire in the Act IV trial. The second part of the scene, which features the enumeration of Sir Pol's harebrained business plans, offers a nice contrast to the schemes of Volpone, Mosca and the legacy hunters. Similar to the Venetians, the English Sir Pol dreams of striking it rich; however, his designs are benign and ineffectual. Finally, Peregrine's dramatic reading of Sir Pol's diary amuses with its banality. It offers a close-up look into the life of a self-important man whose days consist of little more than urinating and the purchasing of toothpicks. Even though this scene is far from the play's best, it still passes the time while humorously cutting the tension and giving a 17th-century English audience (if not a contemporary one) a point of entry as it encounters a foreign civilization and value system. Whether this is enough to justify its presence in the play has been and will continue to be a point of contention.

Act IV, scene ii

1–9 From the moment Sir Pol appears in the previous scene, Lady Would-be's return to the stage becomes inevitable. When we last saw her, she was departing Volpone's home in a huff and had set off in search of her ill-fated husband. Her entrance here does not disappoint, as the passage of time has done little to abate her anger. Trailed by her two beleaguered attendants and the diminutive Nano, Lady Would-be arrives itching for a fight. The chase and the heat have taken their toll on her body, though. The makeup caking her face is melting off in globs. If possible, she has become even more physically repulsive than she was in her encounter with Volpone. Spotting her prey, she girds herself for battle; however, she has made two terrible mistakes: her husband is not cheating, and the woman that she thinks he is with is a man. Jonson has set the stage perfectly for a classic comic misunderstanding built upon misinformation and mistaken identity.

10–58 Oblivious to his wife's disheveled appearance and indignant demeanor, Sir Pol heralds Lady Would-be's arrival by praising her behavior, beauty and discourse. In his exuberance, he invites Peregrine to 'use' her as he wishes. This invitation, which takes on a different connotation when Lady Would-be repeats it, paves the way for an even more disastrous comic misunderstanding in the following scene. Despite Sir Pol's initial enthusiasm, this exchange belongs to Lady Would-be. Although she attempts to maintain some semblance of decorum in the first half of this beat, her façade steadily dissolves until her misplaced rage is left naked and bare as she hurls a slew of insults ('land-siren', 'hermaphrodite', 'lewd harlot', 'base fricatrice' and 'female devil in a male outside') at the bemused Peregrine. This furious invective continues Lady Would-be's pattern of speaking in lists. Remarkably, the gullible Sir Pol is taken in by her slander, and he also comes to believe that Peregrine is female. This 'discovery' prompts him to flee the young man's company and is yet another example of a character (Peregrine in this instance) being defined by the words and labels that describe him/her and not by his/her essential identity. In the trial this phenomenon will play out with much more dire consequences.

59 to the end Sir Pol's abrupt departure sets the stage for a delightful confrontation between Lady Would-be and Peregrine. While Lady Would-be's malapropisms and nonsensical accusations amuse, the real joy of this altercation comes from the physical assault that takes place. Two lines suggest that the situation, following Sir Pol's exit, escalates beyond insults. At line 63 Lady Would-be vows to discipline Peregrine, and at line 67 Peregrine accuses Lady Would-be of attempting 'to beg shirts' (i.e., pulling off his clothing). When staged, this leads to Lady Would-be desperately struggling to undress Peregrine in an attempt to prove he is a woman. This action then begins the second comic misunderstanding at the heart of the subplot: Peregrine's belief that Sir Pol is offering Lady Would-be's sexual services to him.

Act IV, scene iii

1 to the end Mosca's arrival awkwardly interrupts the struggle between Peregrine and Lady Would-be. (One cannot help but wonder what compromising position he discovers them in as he enters. The possibilities for a director are endless.) Mosca's return to the stage also functions as the bridge between the subplot and the central storyline. Just as Mosca forces Lady Would-be out of the main plot and into the subplot by sending her off in search of Sir Pol in Act III, here he brings her out of the B story and back into the A story by requesting her testimony against Celia, Sir Pol's 'actual' mistress. Stunned by this turn of events, Lady Would-be utters what could be a fitting epigraph for the entire play: 'Is't possible? How has my judgement wandered!' In a play about the inability of men and women to see things for what they truly are, Lady Would-be's incredulity is a one-line summation of all that has transpired and will transpire in *Volpone*. After regaining her bearings, she seeks to make amends with Peregrine the only way that she knows how: by offering her grotesque body to him. The comic misunderstanding then reaches its zenith with Peregrine's erroneous deduction that Sir Pol is pimping his wife. This twisted love triangle is a comic inversion of the love triangle between Celia, Corvino and Volpone. In that relationship the reluctant wife (Celia) is forcefully prostituted by her husband (Corvino) to a lecherous man (Volpone). In this relationship, however, it is the wife (Lady Would-be) who prostitutes herself, and it is the husband (Sir Pol) who is mistaken for a bawd by a man (Peregrine) who wants nothing more than to avoid sexual contact with the lady of the house. Thus, Jonson masterfully uses the subplot to reinforce the recurrent motif of inversion in the play.

Act IV, scene iv

1 to the end With the secondary characters dispatched to the wings, the play resumes its primary storyline. Mosca has successfully enlisted the help of the three legacy hunters in Volpone's trial. All that remains is to get everyone on the same page before the court proceedings begin. What makes this scene theatrically compelling is Mosca's juggling act. Mosca needs to reassure each legacy hunter that none of the other coconspirators will reap the benefits of the group's perjury, but Mosca needs to accomplish this while in full view of all three men. It is a delicate situation because the whole plan will collapse if any of the three criminals suspects Mosca of deception. One useful way to think of this scene is as a piece of music in a larger score. Throughout the play Mosca functions as a siren, seducing each of the legacy hunters with a different song about the path to wealth. With the various melodies established in earlier scenes, the composition now becomes more complicated as Mosca tries to 'sing' all three tunes simultaneously. The result is that the audience hears and recognizes the same melodies (i.e., lies) that it has heard previously, but it experiences the music differently because the melodies are interacting with one another, creating a more complicated and chaotic composition. Thus, this scene harkens back to earlier scenes while still propelling the plot forward and giving the audience a feeling of dramatic movement. This technique allows Jonson, as a 'composer' of plays, to craft a scene that feels simultaneously familiar and new.

Act IV, scene v

1–21 This short exchange is a fitting prologue to the trial. It offers several tidbits of information that set the stage for the court proceedings while also creating a false set of expectations about the verdict. The *Avocatori*, who function here as magistrates even though their historic function was as prosecutors (Jonson seems to have misunderstood certain aspects of the Venetian judicial system), appear predisposed toward Celia and Bonario. They presume Volpone's guilt even before the legal process has begun, exposing their bias and casting doubt on the justice of their subsequent rulings. Not only does the opening conversation between the *Avocatori* discredit them and the law in the eyes of the audience, but it also gives viewers the false sense that the play is approaching its conclusion and that Volpone will soon receive his deserved punishment. Thus, in a swift 11 lines Jonson takes a swipe at legal institutions while setting his audience up for an unexpected turn of events. It is a masterfully cynical introduction to a brand of justice that will continue to reveal its moral bankruptcy over the ensuing beats. The second half of this beat leads the audience to expect something else: the imminent arrival of Volpone. By summoning Volpone to appear before the court, the *Avocatori* lay the groundwork for the trial's climax.

Everyone in the audience now anticipates the fox's next trick, and all of the testimony before Volpone's arrival, we expect, will merely be a prelude to the star's performance.

22–102 The progression of the trial is straightforward. It begins with an opening statement by the defense. Following the opening remarks, multiple witnesses speak on behalf of the defendant. The accusers then present their case before the trial concludes with the defense's closing argument and the verdict. In many ways, the structure of this sequence is not that different from the structure of modern trial scenes found on television and film. This makes it arguably the most recognizable scene to a contemporary audience; however, the familiar order of the trial is belied by the moral anarchy that governs the proceedings. What on the surface looks like a typical day in court could not be more atypical, as the guilty are rewarded and the innocent are punished. The engine behind this turn of events is Voltore, who up until this moment has been the most forgettable of the three legacy hunters. Corbaccio is defined by his senility and Corvino by his cruelty; but before his courtroom theatrics, Voltore is an enigma, a vanilla figure who disappears for nearly two acts. What do we even know about him? Unlike Corbaccio and Corvino, he seems to have no relations. This insulates him from the trap that the other legacy hunters fall into. Other than that, he remains vague and undefined. The approximate 40 lines of text that Voltore utters in the first three and a half acts of the play are far less than the number of lines that he speaks in this one beat. For the first time, the audience sees the true Voltore, and what they witness is a formidable lawyer whose forked tongue is as skilled as Mosca's. Almost immediately he takes the judges in, casting doubt on the character of Bonario and Celia with accusations that are as substantive as air. It is worth noting the vividness of Voltore's vocabulary. Imagistic words such as 'treachery', 'impudence', 'vicious', 'malice' and 'wicked' are attached to the hapless Bonario and Celia. In marked contrast, the words linked to Volpone and those prepared to testify on his behalf are 'aged', 'innocent', 'tender' and 'grace'. In short, Voltore harnesses the incredible power of language to refashion the identity of Bonario and Celia before our very eyes. By the time he has concluded his evisceration of Bonario's and Celia's character, the pair can do nothing to rehabilitate their image. In the minds of the listeners, they have become the things that are said about them. Celia recognizes this, and her heartfelt plea for death demonstrates that she sees the handwriting on the wall.

103–14 The first of the crooks to testify is Corbaccio; however, unlike the testimony that follows, Corbaccio's statements do not necessarily qualify as intentional perjury. In III.ix Mosca convinces Corbaccio that Bonario threatened to commit patricide, and so Corbaccio's statements to the court are nothing more than a retelling of a lie that he believes is true. This makes him both a victim of the conspiracy as well as a willing conspirator. This contradiction makes it difficult for the audience to respond to Corbaccio with the same level of indignation and enmity that they have for the other collaborators. In fact, Corbaccio's testimony is somewhat heartbreaking since we see Bonario's enduring loyalty to his father. Unlike Corvino and Celia, whose relationship never approximated something tender, there is a sense that Corbaccio and Bonario were once a loving family before senility set in and warped Corbaccio's personality and values. And of course, Corbaccio's appearance before the court would not be complete without yet another example of his senescence. Corbaccio's inability to correctly hear the questions posed to him breaks the solemnity of the trial and infuses it with a brief yet telling moment of comic ridiculousness. In short, Corbaccio's 11-line testimony is anything but simple. Its tone is layered, and the relationships are complex. The result is that the viewer does not know whether to laugh, cry or shout in protest.

115–34 The next to testify is Corvino. It is worth noting that the order in which the legacy hunters speak before the court parallels the order in which they first appear before Volpone in Act I. This further endows the play with a structural elegance that is typical for Jonson's work and atypical for the period.

Of all the things that Corvino does in his misguided attempt to win Volpone's favor, this testimony is probably the most personally challenging. While sending his wife into Volpone's bedroom must have triggered feelings of jealousy and possessiveness, it remained a private act that brought no embarrassment to Corvino. His statements to the court, however, are a public proclamation of his shame and sexual failings as a man. Under oath Corvino admits, albeit falsely, to being cuckolded by his wife. In doing so, he brings to fruition his deepest fear: the public and humiliating loss of his masculinity. Undoubtedly this is a difficult moment for him. The motivating power of money spurs him on, but it seems like Corvino must also demonstrate a certain amount of reluctance when declaring himself a betrayed husband. His appeal to Mosca for reassurance at line 127 confirms this. Despite the difficulties associated with his testimony, Corvino also sees this situation as an opportunity to engage in his favorite pastime: the vicious castigating and excoriating of his wife. Abandoning any sense of decorum, he becomes so agitated that the court has to halt his testimony. Corvino's outburst also leads to Celia fainting. Thus, in a very short time the excitable Corvino creates chaos in the court, a chaos that underscores a larger loss of control by the inept *Avocatori*.

135 to the end Following Corvino's eruption and Celia's swooning, the proceedings become more hectic. The *Avocatori* dispense with protocol, no longer inquiring if the witnesses have taken an oath, and instead they begin questioning them immediately. Very briefly, Mosca explains the wound he received at the hands of Bonario, but in uncharacteristic fashion he mostly holds his tongue and lets the wound speak for itself. The remainder of the beat is taken up by the continued assassination of Celia's character while the court is primed for the testimony of Lady Would-be. In many ways this beat is alarmingly contemporary and shows how little has changed in the Western world's approach to sex crimes. Although Jonson frequently draws the ire of feminist scholars, the court proceedings in *Volpone* have a strikingly feminist slant, critiquing legal institutions that put the victim on trial. Given all the humor in the play and the chaos of the preceding moments, it is easy to forget that the court is convening because an attempted rape has taken place and that the innocent victim is currently being discredited by a pack of liars and a shrewd lawyer. Called a 'whore', 'harlot' and 'prostitute', Celia is forced to look on silently as others call into question her chastity and integrity by inventing an alternate sexual history for her. Today we refer to this phenomenon as 'slut shaming', and it is an all too frequent presence in modern courtrooms where rape victims must justify everything from their wardrobe to choice of sexual partners. If a production can sift through the theatrics of the trial and remind its audience of the gravity of the moment, then this sequence has the potential to be a powerful form of social commentary.

Act IV, scene vi

1–14 Lady Would-be's testimony progresses as one might expect. In contrast to the previous beat, which is unsettling and grave, Lady Would-be returns *Volpone* to the more comfortable world of comedy. In customary fashion her statements are littered with misunderstandings and an incorrect usage of the English language. The most glaring example of this is her confusion of crocodiles' tears with hyenas' laughter. The comedy of her appearance before the court is enhanced by her habit of speaking without listening. Just as Volpone tried fruitlessly to put an end to Lady Would-be's prattle in Act III, the *Avocatori* also struggle to get a word in. Their statements are limited to a maximum of four words before Lady Would-be interrupts them (note the shared lines in the beat) and resumes making her point. Like Corbaccio's testimony, the incongruity between the humor of Lady Would-be's testimony and the seriousness of the trial engenders a conflicted response in the audience, as it must decide whether to laugh at or mourn the injustice of the situation. Any production, too, must resolve this tension. It can choose to accentuate the comedy associated with the characters and their idiosyncrasies, or it can highlight the tragedy inherent in the situation. The most skillful productions, however, will preserve the complexity of Jonson's work by doing both simultaneously.

14–20 In marked contrast to the passionate perjury of the legacy hunters, Bonario and Celia marshal no arguments in their defense. They are painfully alone in their goodness and have no one who can vouch for them, but why do they not at least speak on their own behalf? Perhaps they are simply in shock and have not regained their bearings after the unexpected ambush by Voltore and his minions. It is also possible that in their naiveté they believe the truth is defense enough. One additional interpretation is that they object to the entire proceedings on principle. They have no respect for a court that has shown itself to be morally bankrupt, and so they protest through silence. Whatever the reason for their passivity, they do little to earn the respect of the *Avocatori* or the audience by remaining mute. Their misguided belief that their consciences and a 'heaven that never fails the innocent' will somehow extricate them from this situation alienates Bonario and Celia from those who might otherwise prove sympathetic to their plight. (This is especially true of a modern audience that finds it theologically difficult to embrace the concept of an interventionist deity.) By outsourcing their defense and potential salvation, Bonario and Celia show themselves to be devoid of any self-reliance. This kind of passivity makes it easy to see why the two are so frequently victimized.

20–53 Although his arrival is unnecessary to secure an acquittal, Volpone's appearance before the court is nevertheless the climax of a trial filled with feats of showmanship and deceit. It is also arguably Volpone's greatest performance in the play. He knows the stakes and understands the consequences of a slip-up. In coming before the court, he masquerades as a mute, impotent and limp rag of a human. In many ways Volpone's performance in this moment is reminiscent of a puppet show, a device that Jonson uses more extensively in the climax of his later play *Bartholomew Fair*. Presumably, Voltore manipulates Volpone's lifeless limbs as he indicates them in his closing argument. In short, Volpone becomes a prop of the puppet master Voltore, and yet at the same time Volpone manipulates the action through his feigned powerlessness. It is a strange paradox that creates all sorts of confusion about who is and who is not in control at any given moment in the play. Adding to the ambiguity and intrigue is the fact that Voltore and the other legacy hunters actually believe that Volpone is as sick as he appears and therefore innocent of the crimes he has been charged with. Thus, while Voltore, Corvino, Corbaccio and Lady Would-be lie, they do so having only a partial awareness of the truth. It is worth keeping this in mind as we assess each character's culpability in this sham of a trial.

54–63 To no one's surprise the *Avocatori* proclaim the acquittal of Volpone and the condemnation of Bonario and Celia. Despite the inevitability of this ruling by the trial's end, the extreme reversal of the *Avocatori* – yet another of *Volpone*'s inversions – is difficult to comprehend. At the opening of the trial, they declare the virtue of Bonario and Celia, but by its conclusion the *Avocatori* mourn their inability to sentence the monstrous pair to death. In short, their vitriolic and intemperate responses are hardly befitting of a profession that requires dispassionate objectivity. The *Avocatori* seem governed by irrational sentiment, and their rulings are more reactionary than well-reasoned judgments. Jonson's most stinging indictment of them and the judicial system that they represent comes when they thank Voltore for his 'worthy service to the state'. In this statement of gratitude, the *Avocatori* demonstrate the complete contamination of Venetian civilization and government. Perhaps Jonson meant merely to contrast the corruption of Venice with the virtue of England; however, it is just as reasonable to read and stage this scene as a commentary on all of mankind's judicial systems no matter the location.

63 to the end   Following the verdict a strange mood pervades the stage. Allies in the trial, the legacy hunters again find themselves adversaries; and Mosca, as before, must convince each that s/he is the favored heir. A palpable feeling of distrust exists among the characters as they probably cast sideways glances at their rivals; nevertheless, each continues to trust blindly in Mosca and the certainty of his/her success. What is odd and almost jarring about this beat is how quickly the crisis of the trial dissipates and the characters revert back to their old concerns. It seems as if the trial was merely a detour, a minor complication that required resolving before the con can be played to its conclusion. It is a strange ending to the penultimate act, and it leaves the audience with little sense of what the crisis or resolution of the final act will be. Will we even return to the courtroom to see the sentencing of Bonario and Celia? Will wrong be made right at last? If so, how? Or will we simply bear witness to the final duping of the legacy hunters and the triumph of Volpone and Mosca? Unlike traditional comedies that conclude with an inevitable marriage, *Volpone* could still go in several different directions when the play's last act commences. It is a refreshing change for a genre that can often be formulaic.

Act V

Act V, scene i

1 to the end   After coming perilously close to disaster and staring into the abyss of almost certain destruction, Volpone is once again safe at home; however, his triumph is of little comfort to him. Rather than reveling in his victory, our crafty antihero is shaken by the day's events. He requires wine to fortify himself in the aftermath of what must have been a harrowing experience, but even the wine fails to fully satisfy a frightened Volpone who desperately needs a new distraction. As so often happens with Volpone, he becomes restless with the status quo, and this restlessness quickly leads to recklessness. A clue of what is to come appears in line 2 when Volpone confesses his newfound 'dislike with [his] disguise'. For the first time in the play, he no longer wishes to impersonate an invalid. Why? Perhaps the public humiliation of having others think him impotent leaves a bitter taste in Volpone's mouth. It is also possible that his recent experiences have made him acutely aware of his own frailty, prompting him to seek out the guise of a stronger individual (hence, his disguise as a *commandatore* later in the act). Or maybe the perpetually bored fox simply needs something new to entertain him. Whatever the reason, Volpone no longer wishes to continue his turn as a dying man, and this change sets in motion all subsequent events in Act V.

Many have critiqued the final act for featuring events that are not a logical consequence of the previous acts' events. These individuals see Volpone's reversal of fortune as a self-inflicted, manufactured crisis. They argue that the situation resolves itself with Volpone's acquittal in Act IV and that Jonson artificially restarts the play by having Volpone make the unnecessary choice to discard his disguise as an invalid. There is some validity to this argument. Ultimately, the problem stems from the fact that Jonson endeavors to write a moral play about evil men. In classical comedy the central characters begin in a state of equilibrium before being thrown into a state of disequilibrium. This chaos persists until the play's conclusion when all wrongs are righted and the characters return to tranquility. What makes *Volpone* different is that the peace of the play's central characters is at odds with a greater societal peace. When Volpone's life and Mosca's life revert to normalcy at the conclusion of Act IV, it throws the moral world of the play into complete anarchy. If a greater order is to be restored, it must bring disorder to the lives of the play's main characters; and if the play's main characters are to experience stability, then it must create widespread upheaval in the moral universe. This tension prompts Jonson to use rather unorthodox methods, including the artificial crisis in Act V, to satisfactorily resolve the plot of *Volpone*.

Act V, scene ii

1–58 Mosca's return, as it frequently does, rejuvenates Volpone. The isolation and anxiety Volpone experiences dissipate the moment Mosca appears. He is once again gleeful because he has someone with whom he can share his triumph. One of the ironies of Volpone's achievement as an actor is that he can never receive the applause he craves because no one except his inner circle knows that he is acting. Consequently, his performance goes unappreciated and unacknowledged by all save Mosca. Even though Volpone never says so openly, this must eat away at him. It certainly accounts for his intense attachment to Mosca, which is genuine despite his parasite's eventual betrayal. Mosca is the only one who understands Volpone, and in this moment that understanding morphs into a shared delight of their greatest feat. The pair mimic Voltore, laugh at the fate of the two innocents and gloat about their ability to blind both the court and the legacy hunters; yet underneath all this gaiety is a subtle feeling of emptiness. Mosca is ready to rest and retire because he knows that nothing can be done to top their most recent trick. By acknowledging at line 13 that 'this is [their] masterpiece', Mosca is doing more than just celebrating their achievement; he is also coming to grips with the painful reality that everything he and Volpone do from here on out will pale in comparison to this moment. Like an artist after producing his/her masterwork, Mosca and Volpone experience both the ecstasy of excellence and the terror of knowing that they will never equal such a triumph again. Perhaps it is this fear that drives each of them to make a series of ill-conceived decisions in the final act.

58–63 The first of these fateful choices occurs in this short beat when Volpone decides to kill his sickly incarnation. Volpone has clearly not considered what the story looks like if he is no longer in it. He seems to believe that, like a snake, he can shed his worn skin and grow a new skin without complications. He does not anticipate Mosca's betrayal, but even without Mosca's duplicity the staging of his own death is a plan fraught with difficulty. Who does he become and how can he engage with the world if no one believes that he exists? That being said, it is easy to see why Volpone would embark down this path. His disguise has become a prison of sorts. Feeble, impotent and mute as an invalid, Volpone can do little more than spectate while Mosca runs the show. Furthermore, as Mosca notes in the previous beat, there is no way the pair can outdo themselves in this particular con. Thus, killing himself off allows Volpone to have a fresh start, something he desperately craves once he recognizes the pitfalls of his disguise. Finally, he does this because it is the best way to psychologically damage the legacy hunters. While Volpone lives, they still have hope of acquiring a fortune, but Volpone's 'death' means that their dreams will be dashed and their humiliation complete. The convergence of all of these factors prompts Volpone to do the unthinkable and unadvisable: commit 'suicide'.

63 to the end   Volpone's announcement must come as a shock to Mosca. As usual, he takes this new information in stride and keeps his cards close to his vest. Unlike earlier instances, this scheme is entirely Volpone's invention. Typically Mosca implants an idea in a character's head, and then that character comes to believe that s/he is the originator of the idea. In this moment, however, Volpone's plan is entirely his concoction. The irony is that it could not be more beneficial to Mosca had Mosca suggested it himself. The key component of the plot is Volpone's decision to make Mosca his heir. Volpone assumes that this, like everything else in the play, is simply acting. His directive to Mosca to 'put on a gown and take upon thee as thou wert mine heir' demonstrates Volpone's belief that his plan is nothing more than a theatrical exercise. What he fails to grasp is that Mosca will see this situation not as acting but as life. Ultimately, Volpone's fatal flaw is his inability to distinguish between reality and performance.

Act V, scene iii

1–22   Volpone's 'death' is a joyous occasion. Each of the four legacy hunters arrives believing that s/he is poised to inherit tremendous wealth. What makes this scene and the final act work is the reversal of fortune that each character experiences, but that reversal is only apparent if the audience first sees the characters at their greatest heights. For the legacy hunters, that moment is now. All that they have sacrificed – their wealth, their pride, their family and their dignity – is finally paying off as they come to receive their recompense. Their elation should be palpable when they enter this house of death. The beat is a busy one, with one legacy hunter hurriedly arriving after another. As the room becomes more crowded, suspicion and tension grow; yet none of the newly arrived has the slightest inkling of the truth. All of this happens while Mosca inventories Volpone's possessions. He travels from item to item as Voltore, Corbaccio, Corvino and Lady Would-be comically pester him for answers. (Corbaccio's 'Dost thou not hear?' at line 8 is one of the play's most priceless lines.) On the periphery of the action is Volpone, who adopts his preferred role of spectator. In many ways the audience sees this scene from Volpone's perspective. Like Volpone, we want to see the legacy hunters suffer. They are all despicable people who deserve much worse than the fate that Volpone doles out to them. The audience is with Volpone as he eagerly anticipates the moment when the legacy hunters discover who the true heir is, yet it is also bothersome to be allied with such an unsavory character. This is the conundrum of *Volpone*. In a play where no human being is worth rooting for, the audience must identify with the person who represents the least of the evils. More often than not, that individual is Volpone.

22–101 In keeping with dramatic tradition, the final act of *Volpone* is filled with revelations and realizations. The first domino to fall is Voltore's exclamation of 'Mosca the heir!' at line 22. This line sucks all of the air out of the room, fittingly given Volpone's use of the word 'gasp' on the same line. One by one, the legacy hunters discover how they have been cozened. In this beat they come to grasp more than just the mechanism of their downfall, though. They realize who they have become and what they have done in search of wealth. Yes, Mosca reminds them of these things because he knows that the legacy hunters' crimes render them powerless in a court of law, but Mosca's remarks are about much more than that. What Mosca aims to do is instill a sense of shame in Lady Would-be, Corvino, Corbaccio and Voltore. He wants to make them aware of their deepest failings and of all that they have lost in this foolhardy endeavor. For the first time, the legacy hunters apprehend the truth not only about Volpone's fortune but also about themselves, and it strikes them to the core. They are dumb when confronted with the awesome, incontrovertible facts of their own lives.

102 to the end As in prior scenes, we again see the depth of affection that Volpone feels for his parasite. His frequent urge to embrace and kiss Mosca throughout the play is exceptionally revealing and often takes on homoerotic undertones in production. The sexualized language that Volpone uses to describe Mosca ('divine', 'exquisite', etc.) here and elsewhere also suggests some level of attraction. Most telling, though, is Volpone's stated desire at line 104 to 'transform [Mosca] to a Venus', for it shows that Volpone conceives of Mosca as a life partner if his sex were not a barrier. Such is the extent of Volpone's passion for his servant, and perhaps it is the thing that ultimately blinds Volpone to Mosca's treachery. Volpone's fondness for Mosca manifests itself in another way as well: it appears in his wish to remake Mosca in his own image. By dressing up Mosca in his own clothing, Volpone is giving more than just a garment to Mosca. He is handing over his identity as well as all of the power, wealth and status connoted by the gown of the *clarissimo*. Mosca is not the only one receiving a different identity in this scene, though. Volpone, too, acquires a new outfit: the guise of a *commandatore*. It is fitting that both characters, as we approach the moment in the play when their true natures are exposed, continue to don masks and apparel that conceal who they really are.

Act V, scene iv

1–27 Even in productions that preserve the Sir Pol subplot, this scene is frequently cut. By the time this scene occurs, *Volpone* is galloping along toward its conclusion with spectators sensing the evening is almost over, and this scene, which has no bearing on the action of Act V, is a clear roadblock to the resolution of a rather long comedy. Peregrine and Sir Pol's comic interlude at the start of Act II is a refreshing palate cleanser early in the performance, especially for a British audience. The Act IV exchange merges the primary storyline with the subplot, but this particular scene seems to do little more than delay the play's climax. So why is it here? Like IV.i–iii, this scene allows the main storyline to advance offstage without it feeling like the continuity of time has been broken. In addition, it ties up the loose ends in Sir Pol's relationship with Peregrine. If we see the Peregrine-Sir Pol subplot as a self-contained playlet inside a much larger play, then it makes sense to include the final outcome of their encounter. These two reasons, though, are probably not enough to merit the continued presence of this scene in the play's final act. Thus, if we want to find a compelling reason for Jonson's inclusion of this scene, we need to look at the two dominant motifs of the final act: disguise and punishment/torture.

The first line of this scene is 'Am I enough disguised?' This clearly connects to the final nine lines of the previous conversation between Volpone and Mosca, and its construction is almost identical to Volpone's opening line in V.v: 'Am I then like him?' By creating a second narrative in which disguise plays a pivotal role, Jonson makes his characters' fascination with role-playing universal as opposed to contextual. Peregrine's trick demonstrates that the donning of masks is not merely particular to a group of con men in exotic Venice but that it is a part of the human condition, something that we all do irrespective of culture.

27 to the end Although questions about performance and disguise run through the entire play, it is not until the play nears its finish that the nature of justice, punishment and torture becomes a central concern of the work. In fact, the exploration of this theme begins at line 61 in IV.vi: 'You shall hear ere night what punishment the court decrees upon 'em.' From this moment on, the play's primary preoccupation is the penalty for vice. By nightfall each character is held accountable for his/her behavior, but these accountings straddle the line between justice and torture and leave the audience wondering whether the characters truly receive the punishments that they deserve. One character who suffers an especially hard fate is Sir Pol. Although Peregrine suspects Sir Pol of prostituting Lady Would-be, in actuality his crime is nothing more than excessive stupidity and a poor choice of a mate. For this he is violently beaten and publicly humiliated. What is so striking about this scene is its cruelty. Peregrine's men jump on and strike Sir Pol's shell. They even ponder rolling a cart over it. Peregrine commands Sir Pol to creep like a cowardly animal, stripping him of all personal dignity. Although there is a certain amount of comedy inherent in the scene's stage business, its savagery demonstrates the inability of men to dole out an appropriate punishment to the appropriate person. Sadly for Sir Pol, he endures all of the fates later inflicted upon Mosca (physical punishment), Volpone (confinement), Corvino (public humiliation), Corbaccio (banishment/exile) and Voltore (loss of a profession). Whether this interesting parallel, along with the aforementioned disguise connection, is enough to justify prolonging the evening is something that each director will have to decide as s/he considers the audience's attention span and the overall aims of the production.

Act V, scene v

1 to the end At the top of this scene, Volpone and Mosca are playing dress-up. Appearing as a *commandatore* (i.e., an Italian court officer), Volpone now assumes his fourth persona of the play. (Earlier characters are the invalid, Scoto of Mantua and the dashing lover.) In contrast to the frequently costumed and heavily made-up Volpone, Mosca is dressing up for the first time. Mosca's typical aversion to disguise should be a tipoff that he considers his habit of the *clarissimo* (i.e., Venetian gentleman) to be a new reality, not a costume. Oblivious to the differences in their attitudes toward costuming, Volpone assumes that he and Mosca are engaging in the same activity; but Mosca does not play dress-up, something that becomes abundantly clear after his master exits.

The five-line exchange between Volpone and Mosca at the top of the scene sticks out like a sore thumb. Almost every scene in the play features a protracted back and forth between the characters, but this exchange's striking brevity and expository nature make one question the necessity of it. Perhaps the shortness of the scene can be used to indicate that a fundamental alteration in the relationship between Volpone and Mosca has occurred; however, a cleaner edit of the play would cut the first six lines of this scene and move Mosca's V.v speech, beginning with 'I'll make him languish...', to the end of V.iii after Volpone's exit. If one also cuts the Peregrine-Sir Pol interlude, then it makes for a rapid yet doable costume change for Volpone. The result, though, is a streamlined final act with a swift resolution.

As for Mosca's betrayal of Volpone, why does he do it? When does he decide to do it? It is impossible to answer one question without answering the other. Perhaps double-crossing Volpone is Mosca's endgame from the start. Such a reading forces one to interpret all of Mosca's earlier decisions, starting with his mention of Celia in I.v, as a sinister trap designed to ensnare his master. It is equally possible that Mosca is simply an opportunist who sees the tremendous gain to be had only after Volpone designates him his heir. In this reading Volpone's wealth is not something that Mosca actively seeks out from the beginning but something that is too good to pass up once it becomes available. A third way of viewing Mosca's treachery is as a gradual event. In this interpretation Mosca becomes increasingly frustrated with Volpone's antics and risky decisions. The trial and its accompanying danger serve as a wake-up call for Mosca, who decides to sever ties with Volpone once it becomes clear that Volpone's reckless decisions are imperiling Mosca's own well-being. It would be foolish to say that one view is superior to another. All can be reasonably argued. The important thing is for an actor to make a clear choice that guides his interactions with Volpone throughout the production.

Act V, scene vi

1 to the end Despite being divided into four scenes, V.vi–ix can be thought of as one continuous, rapid sequence with a single central action: the fox's mockery of the gulled legacy hunters. As frequently occurs in beast fables, the fox's ridicule of his adversaries causes his downfall; however, Volpone's mockery of Corvino, Corbaccio and Voltore acquires an added layer of irony now that we know Volpone, too, has been deceived and cheated by Mosca. He is no longer a winner taunting a bunch of losers; instead, he is an unknowing loser acting like a victor. This dramatic irony gives the audience a perverse pleasure as they watch Volpone unwittingly humiliate himself, and it produces a very different response in viewers than Volpone's gloating in V.iii, which occurs before we know that Volpone has been double-crossed by his parasite.

Act V, scene vii

1 to the end Voltore's separation from Corvino and Corbaccio is a harbinger of things to come. Although the audience has no inkling of what will transpire during the sentencing, the fact that the three legacy hunters are not on stage together is a subtle hint that a rift has occurred or will soon occur among them. In marked contrast to IV.iv, where the legacy hunters appear simultaneously and are a united front before the first court sequence, the arrangement of V.vi–ix shows that Corvino and Corbaccio remain a unit while Voltore, as evidenced by his separate entrances and exits, has broken off from the group even before the second court sequence begins.

In this short scene, Volpone teases Voltore by appearing as a suitor for his newfound 'wealth'. The mockery is twofold. First, by requesting financial favors from the advocate, Volpone reminds Voltore of his financial failure. Beyond this superficial level is a reminder that Voltore, too, was once a suitor of Volpone's fortune. Thus, when Volpone petitions Voltore for a portion of Volpone's 'inheritance', it is a convoluted request filled with layers of meaning that Voltore is oblivious to.

Act V, scene viii

1 to the end With each French scene in this sequence, the speed and the intensity of the action increase. Between V.vii and V.viii, Volpone must race to the next corner so that he can again head off Corvino and Corbaccio before they arrive at court. This dash should create a frenetic feel as the almost manic Volpone looks to land one last jab before the sentencing begins. He is truly a man incapable of walking away from the game, and this inability causes him a series of problems throughout the final act, including in this scene. Ratcheting up the intensity of the scene is Mosca, whose silent appearance further agitates Corvino and Corbaccio by reminding them of the blessed fate that was almost theirs. It is very important that the actors playing Corvino, Corbaccio and Voltore not get too upset too early in this sequence, for if they blow a gasket in V.vi or V.vii, they leave themselves nowhere to go as the events progress and the insults accumulate. By line 18, though, the hotheaded Corvino reaches a breaking point and goes after Volpone. This altercation is reminiscent of the beating that Volpone receives from Corvino in II.iii; however, Volpone has clearly learned his lesson from the earlier confrontation with Corvino and does his best to evade the merchant's attack. The sequence, which should feature a good chase around the stage, is an amusing bit of physical comedy; and as happens frequently in *Volpone*, the play's title character only escapes trouble thanks to the timely arrival of Mosca.

Act V, scene ix

1 to the end With Corvino and Corbaccio dispatched, Voltore now returns to the stage. Like Corvino and Corbaccio, Voltore becomes even more enraged after his encounter with Mosca. This carries over into his subsequent exchange with Volpone, which is even more heated than V.vii. The question of this scene is when does Voltore decide that he will change his story to the court. In line 22 of V.xi, Volpone implies it is his mockery of Voltore that ultimately drives the lawyer to change his story ('When I provoked [the advocate], then I lost myself.'), but is Volpone's understanding of the situation accurate or convenient revisionism? If Volpone is correct, then the arc of the sequence is clear. Voltore is steadily driven to exasperation; as a result, he arrives at the court and makes a kneejerk decision to blow up the entire story that he concocted with Mosca, Corvino and Corbaccio. In this interpretation Voltore's subsequent choices are the logical consequence of receiving one too many insults from the relentless Volpone. There is, however, another way of seeing the situation. It is possible that Voltore, even before his entrance in V.vii, has already decided that his only hope is to rat out Mosca. This would explain his opening remark to Mosca: 'It is summer with you now; your winter will come on.' Such an interpretation changes the dynamic between Volpone and Voltore. It means that the interaction between the two of them is more controlled and that Volpone is more of an irritant than a catalyst for Voltore's decision to take Mosca down.

Act V, scene x

1–20 The final act of *Volpone* can be divided into four sections: the 'death' of Volpone and reading of the will (V.i–iii), the humiliation of Sir Pol (V.iv), the mockery of the legacy hunters (V.v–ix) and the sentencing of the criminals (V.x–xii). In contrast to the first four acts, all of which take place in either one or two locations, the final act features scenes in four different locations. Although a subtle change, the multiple locations allude to the mounting chaos in the characters' lives. Events progress too rapidly and in too many places for the characters to keep tabs on all that is happening, and inevitably the wheels come off.

The beginning of the end is Voltore's confession. Like many of the developments in the second courtroom sequence, Voltore's confession is a mixture of clarity and confusion. It is also the first of several events that have a virtuous result despite nefarious motivations. This tension between a moral outcome and an immoral process is the defining feature of the play's final scenes, and it leaves viewers feeling ambivalent about all that transpires. Throughout his confession Voltore uses religious language, including the words 'conscience' (used three times in seven lines), 'prostrate', 'mercy' and 'justice'. Even Celia attributes this turn of events to heaven (something that she or Bonario will do two more times before the play concludes), but the truth is that Voltore is motivated by nothing more than spite, jealousy and opportunity. As his subsequent reversal in V.xii demonstrates, Voltore experiences no remorse. He is simply looking for a way to undo Mosca and gain access to Volpone's fortune. Thus, Voltore's speech to the court, like nearly everything else in the play, is a calculated performance. The difference is that this performance also contains elements of truth within it, and it is this partial truth that brings more confusion than the bald-faced lies of earlier scenes.

20 to the end Following Volpone's exit, the situation becomes even murkier. Corvino and Voltore become adversaries while the *Avocatori* function as mediators attempting to decipher the truth. What is so striking in this beat is the unabashed corruption and almost cartoonish stupidity of the *Avocatori*. Although this theme will be developed more substantially in V.xii, this scene shows how Mosca's newfound wealth has altered the court's opinion of him. They now defer to him and offer him preferential treatment because of the great estate that he has inherited. Thus, Jonson shows that justice for the rich and justice for the poor are entirely different. This insight into the relationship between privilege and justice is one of many that make *Volpone* as relevant today as it was in 1606. The *Avocatori* are more than just corrupt, though. They are embarrassingly inept. It would be a terrible mistake to play these roles dryly or stodgily. Not only does such a representation miss Jonson's satire, it is also much less theatrically compelling than a group of comic buffoons huddling together as they try fruitlessly to uncover the truth.

The other intriguing aspect of this beat is the fact that none of the legacy hunters consciously dissembles. While they contradict each other (Corbaccio even contradicts himself), everything that they utter, excepting Corvino's assertion that Volpone has died, is factually accurate. All of the lies have made the reality of the situation so convoluted that the truth only further complicates things. More than anything else, this beat demonstrates Jonson's belief that the truth is far from simple. It can even contain contradictory yet not mutually exclusive propositions. Through this scene Jonson breaks down facile, binary understandings of things such as good and evil, truth and falsehood; and instead he shows how it is possible for something to be simultaneously good and evil, true and untrue.

Act V, scene xi

1 to the end In traditional tragedy the protagonist of the work experiences a moment of recognition that coincides with his/her reversal of fortune. This recognition is a discrete event that acts as a clear dividing line in the play: there is the protagonist before the recognition and the protagonist after the recognition. Following this moment, the protagonist then suffers greatly for his/her errors. *Volpone* contains all three of these elements; however, Volpone's moment of recognition/reversal of fortune is not one discrete event: it is a gradual unfolding that begins in this scene and concludes only when he decides to uncase himself in the following scene. At the top of V.xi, Volpone finally comprehends the role that he has played in his own downfall. He realizes that his inability to accept his good fortune and walk away from the game while he was still ahead is the reason he now finds himself in such a difficult predicament. For the first time in the play, he understands the danger of his fancies; and rightly or wrongly, he believes that his provocations are the reason Voltore recants before the court. Despite having a clearer sense of his own shortcomings, Volpone still fails to see Mosca for who he truly is. When Nano and Androgyno inform Volpone of Mosca's betrayal, Volpone enters into a state of disbelief. At line 18 he says that '[Mosca's] meaning may be truer than my fear'. He is clearly in a state of denial about his beloved parasite. Like anyone who has been cheated, Volpone finds it impossible to accept that he could be so stupid or that someone he loved and trusted could be so duplicitous.

Eventually, Volpone will be forced to admit the undeniable truth about Mosca, but for now he is only capable of experiencing a partial recognition. He can hold the mirror up to himself, yet he cannot do the same to his partner in crime.

Act V, scene xii

1–10 In marked contrast to Volpone, who has just experienced a moment of clarity, the *Avocatori* are as perplexed as ever. What were they doing while Volpone was having his revelation? Were they in a frozen tableau while the lights switched to Volpone elsewhere on the stage? Were they futilely perusing legal documents in full view of the audience while Corvino protested this turn of events? Did their confusion and frustration steadily increase during this activity? It is a strange and maybe even singular occurrence in the play to have simultaneous scenes occurring in different spaces, and it creates a dilemma in production. Does one suspend the action while Volpone speaks and then resume it again at the top of V.xii, or does one simply let the action in the court continue silently through gesture while Volpone speaks? If one chooses the latter, then it could pull focus from Volpone's speech; however, if one chooses the former, then it might make for a jarring break in a play that is otherwise incredibly fluid. Either way, transitioning out of and back into the court sequence requires some creative problem solving.

Once the legal proceedings resume, events pick up with Corvino's repeated claim that Voltore is possessed. Throughout *Volpone* religious imagery and language abound. Characters are frequently linked with either heaven (Celia's name even means 'heavenly one') or hell, but these ideas seem to proliferate significantly in the play's waning moments, making it difficult to deny *Volpone*'s connection to the morality plays of the Middle Ages. The irony of Corvino's claim is that Voltore's revised testimony, despite being motivated by greed and malice, is still his most virtuous act in the play; nevertheless, Corvino sees madness and the devil in it, for he cannot comprehend why someone would seemingly act against his self-interest. In short, the entire situation is yet another example of a world turned upside down, a world in which speaking the truth becomes the devil's work.

11–49 This beat is one of the most difficult beats to pull off credibly in a modern production. Two events in this beat test the audience's willing suspension of disbelief. The first moment is Voltore's immediate acceptance of Volpone's claim that Mosca was merely jesting. Unlike most of the other characters in the play, Voltore is not a stupid individual. Though his abilities are not equal to Volpone's or Mosca's, he is no slouch either (something his performance in the trial demonstrates). Why, then, is he so quick to take Volpone at his word? Voltore's trust in Volpone becomes even more inexplicable when one considers their prior interactions. Disguised as a *commandatore*, Volpone did nothing but antagonize and embarrass Voltore, so why would Voltore now find this very same individual a reliable source of information? Throughout the play characters delude themselves, seeing only what they want to see; however, Voltore's gullibility in this moment is so extreme that it becomes implausible, and it presents a real problem for productions that are committed to preserving verisimilitude. Given the difficulty of rendering Voltore's behavior realistically in this moment, it almost seems advisable to adopt either a farcical or Brechtian approach that comments on the character's actions. If, however, one is committed to preserving the truth of the moment, then the actor playing Voltore must find a compelling reason to accept the *commandatore*'s story. Perhaps that reason is Volpone's allusion to the parasite, for Mosca could conceivably still have such a strong hold on Voltore that he would accept any piece of information that has Mosca as its source.

The second problematic incident in this beat is Voltore's possession. When *Volpone* premiered in 1606, the vast majority of the audience thought that the devil or other evil spirits could possess an individual; therefore, it did not seem incredible that the *Avocatori* would mistake Voltore for a man possessed. In the ensuing centuries, science and reason have made most skeptical of such phenomena. If one is doing a period production, then Voltore's possession is not a problem since a modern audience will simply accept this moment as an accurate depiction of life in an earlier era. If, however, one is doing a modernized production, then this scene can become a little tricky. 'Why', a contemporary audience member may ask, 'would a modern court, even one as obtuse as this, accept such a thing?' It is something for directors to consider as they decide when and where to set their production and how best to translate a 17th-century play into a 21st-century production.

Despite the difficulties associated with Voltore's feigned possession, it is still an incredibly theatrical and amusing moment. The actor portraying Voltore gets to showcase his physical talents as he writhes around on the ground impersonating a man expelling a foreign spirit from his body. As he does this, Volpone leads Corvino and Corbaccio in a detailed description of the spirit's migration. The whole occurrence is yet another example of the creative power of language and suggestion in *Volpone*. By saying that the spirit moves 'in shape of a blue toad with bat's wings', Volpone allows both those on stage and in the audience to see something that is not there. Words are, in fact, making the unreal real.

49–85 With Mosca's appearance everyone is once again in the same room. There is a sense that the chaos will soon be over and that the characters will gain the clarity they seek. For Volpone to escape yet again, he simply needs Mosca to testify that his master is still living. Volpone's opening comment to Mosca suggests that he thinks his parasite will happily accommodate his request, but Volpone does not understand the new reality confronting him. Even after learning of Mosca's treachery in the previous scene, Volpone still clings to the foolish notion that it was all just a misunderstanding. He is quickly stripped of this false optimism, and his moment of recognition is finally complete. He sees Mosca for what he is: a sadistic, self-serving cheat. In many ways, Volpone's realization prompts him to experience all five of Elizabeth Kübler-Ross' stages of grief in this beat: denial (lines 49–58), anger (lines 58–62), bargaining (lines 63–73), depression (lines 73–82) and acceptance (lines 82–5). Volpone's response runs the gamut of emotions because Mosca's betrayal is personal and produces a profound sense of loss that goes above and beyond the pain of a lost fortune.

As for Mosca, he clearly overplays his hand. He thinks that Volpone, like the other legacy hunters, will never betray him because to do so would be impractical, but the pragmatic Mosca makes a common mistake: he assumes that others, when confronted with a difficult situation, will respond in the same way that he will. Volpone, however, is driven by more than just self-interest. He is motivated by spite. Behavioral economists have shown that while most individuals make decisions from a place of rational self-interest, there is still a substantial group of people who opt to punish those behaving badly even when doing so goes against one's best interest. Volpone is just such a person. He would rather see everyone suffer than suffer alone even if it means an increase in his own hardship. When one couples Volpone's philosophy with the fact that at this point he does not have much left to lose, it becomes obvious why he would out himself in court.

It is also possible to approach this beat from a less serious or psychological vantage point. The psychological perspective is quite useful if one sees *Volpone* as a high-stakes drama full of backstabbing and deceit, but if one treats the play as lighthearted material, then the essence of this beat is Volpone's impetuousness and childishness. In this reading Volpone is not motivated by complex emotions such as grief and loss but by pettiness. An actor who subscribes to this interpretation would present the audience with an embittered Volpone who simply makes a kneejerk decision without fully comprehending the consequences of his action. Volpone's rashness would also quicken the pace of the scene while lessening the gravity of the situation. Although this approach is lacking in drama, it is truer to the spirit of comedy and underscores the ridiculousness of the entire situation. Ultimately, a director has three choices in this beat: s/he can give the audience psychological realism, zany comedy or a blend of the two.

85–102 The climactic moment in *Volpone* is the fox's uncasing. With one act of disrobing, Volpone unties the knot that has perplexed the *Avocatori* and clouded the truth. If the previous beat was Volpone's personal moment of recognition, then this beat represents the moment of recognition for everyone else on stage. At last, the characters understand the trick that has been played on them. How do they react to this discovery? Corbaccio and Voltore, both of whom are silent in this beat, appear dumbstruck (although it is reasonable to question whether Corbaccio has even heard Volpone's confession correctly). The flabbergasted Mosca and Corvino seem to protest this turn of events. The *Avocatori*, Bonario and Celia welcome this revelation as a miracle and act of heaven. The real star of this beat, though, is Volpone. What does he look like when he finally shows his true form? Throughout the play the audience gets periodic glimpses of what appears to be 'the authentic Volpone', but have we truly seen him as he is? If so, then this moment loses some of its power. It simply becomes the moment when the characters catch up to the audience, but what if it is possible to surprise the audience in this moment as well? What if this is a new incarnation of the fox? Can the audience see a Volpone that they did not know existed? It is an interesting challenge, especially for a costume and make-up designer; but if met, it could do much to eliminate what might otherwise be an anticlimactic end to the play.

103 to the end Following the moment of recognition comes the suffering and doling out of 'justice'. It is remarkable how the conclusion of *Volpone* straddles the line between traditional comedy and tragedy. There is almost a marriage (Mosca and the daughter of the fourth *Avocatore*), as would be the case in a traditional comedy; however, the play, which is undeniably a comedy, ends with the customary conclusion of tragedy: physical and psychological torment. The punishment begins when Mosca is forced to forfeit the garments of a gentleman. The sentencing then proceeds in an orderly manner. Each character's fate is carefully tailored to his crime. Mosca, the sadist, must suffer a public beating. Volpone, who is perpetually in motion, will be locked in place; and his fortune, which he amassed through the ridicule of the sick, will be donated to a hospital. Voltore, whose only enjoyment is the law, forfeits his right to practice his profession. Corbaccio, who never once considers the morality of his actions, is made to sit in contemplation in a monastery. And Corvino, who fears public shame above all else, must endure just that. However, as with earlier moments in the courtroom, there is something incongruous and unsatisfying about the approach of the *Avocatori*. Celia's appeal for mercy is treated as a stain on her character, and Mosca suffers a harsher punishment than Volpone simply because of his social rank. What are we to make of all this? If we take the final three lines of the play at face value, then the whole proceedings are nothing more than a straightforward admonition to avoid greed in its most noxious excess; but if we consider the messenger, one of the *Avocatori*, then the message becomes significantly more complex. How are we supposed to trust a moral message from a morally bankrupt man and institution? It is the perfect ending to a complicated play masquerading as a simple parable.

Epilogue

1 to the end   The epilogue, if kept, presents the same dilemma that the prologue does: is it the character speaking or is it the actor? If it is the character, then it can be treated and staged as one final escape for the fox, a cynical reminder that wiliness always triumphs in the end. If it is the actor playing Volpone, then this is yet another opportunity to highlight the notion of Volpone-as-performer. In essence, such an approach to the epilogue shows that there is no difference between the profession of Volpone and the man playing him. Both stand before a judging audience awaiting an unknown verdict. It is a metatheatrical moment and a chance to add a second uncasing to the production. Volpone's makeup can come off, the houselights can be raised and the last vestiges of theatrical illusion can vanish. It is a gentle reminder to the audience that playtime is over and that cast, character and audience must all return to a far less exciting reality.

4 Key Productions and Performances

A production history serves several functions. Most importantly it reconstructs past performances so that their memory endures even after all who bore witness to a particular performance have died. Unlike film, theater is an ephemeral art form that requires scholars who are committed to preserving records of individual performances. Without the efforts of theater historians, the work of theater artists would perish the moment after the cast takes its final bow. Performance histories also show how attitudes and approaches to a play can evolve and change over time. They demonstrate how various productions can exist in conversation with each other, sometimes borrowing and sometimes intentionally deviating from earlier productions; and they look for ways in which a production is responding to a particular moment in history. Thus, theater historians are not evaluating individual performances in a vacuum, as reviewers often do, but are instead seeing productions as part of a vast historical continuum. Furthermore, because production histories detail the benefits and drawbacks of specific production choices and directorial approaches, they have the potential to influence future practice. Finally, production histories can inform the critical discourse surrounding a particular play. Most academics devote themselves to arguing about the meaning of a text, but production histories force scholars to consider the viability of a particular interpretation in performance; for example, it is one thing to claim that *Volpone* is a proto-Marxist text, but it is something else entirely to do as Joan Littlewood did in 1955 and stage it as such.

In this chapter my goal is to provide readers with a production history of *Volpone* that does more than just reconstruct previous stagings. I want to demonstrate how directorial approaches to *Volpone* have changed since its famous return to the stage in 1921, and I hope that accounts of past productions will give readers a sense of the many ways in which this comedy can and cannot work successfully on the stage. Specific attention will be paid to choices pertaining to characterization, editing, genre (i.e., which productions treat *Volpone* as a farce, which as a satire, which as a tragicomedy, etc.) and design (i.e., which productions set *Volpone* in 17th-century Venice, which in the present, which in a metaphorical or timeless space, etc.). Although all major productions in the 20th and early 21st centuries will be considered, this chapter will focus disproportionately on more recent productions since there is a vast array of scholarly material already devoted to productions of *Volpone* between 1921 and Jonson's quatercentennial in 1972.

Return to repertory: the rediscovery of *Volpone* in the early 20th century

Between 1785 and 1921 there was not a single performance of *Volpone*. As noted in Chapter 1, *Volpone*'s disappearance from the stage was the result of many factors: its length, its studied precision, its cynical and unapologetic depiction of human depravity and its inability to withstand comparisons to the plays of the now universally revered Shakespeare. In 1921, however, *Volpone*'s fortunes began to change when the Phoenix Society, a group committed to reviving forgotten Elizabethan and Jacobean plays, mounted a two-night-only private production at the Lyric Theatre in Hammersmith. Theater historian Rebecca Yearling described the performance as follows:

> This production was heavily influenced by William Poel's revivals of Jacobean plays using original staging and costuming; the set was largely bare and left unchanged throughout the performance, and the text seems to have been uncut. (p. 37)

In attendance were the poets William Butler Yeats and T.S. Eliot. Both responded enthusiastically to the performance. Writing for *The Dial*, Eliot heaped praise upon the Phoenix Society and the production directed by Allan Wade, referring to it as 'the most important theatrical event of the year in London' (p. 158). Although Eliot's account complimented the actors and defended the Phoenix Society's practice of performing texts unedited, the primary purpose of his article was to praise Jonson's 'consummate skill' and to remind readers that Jonson's plays can be produced 'without a moment of tedium from end to end' (p. 158). In short, Eliot recognized that the most important aspect of the Phoenix Society's production of *Volpone* was the text itself and not the individual production choices. More than anything, the Phoenix Society's revival was proof that, contrary to 19th-century belief, *Volpone* could engage audiences and work as a piece of theater. With *Volpone*'s theatrical viability established, the door was now open for subsequent revivals of the play in years to come.

Throughout the 1920s and 30s, *Volpone* was revived intermittently. The Phoenix Society remounted its production for a one-night-only benefit in 1923. That same year the Marlowe Society, an amateur theatrical group, also staged a favorably received production in Cambridge. After a seven-year absence from the stage, *Volpone* was performed at the Cambridge Festival Theatre in 1930, and in 1935 the Birmingham Repertory Theatre produced a heavily cut version of the play. Although these infrequent revivals did just enough to keep *Volpone* alive in the minds of the English public, none made the play anything more than a work of marginal importance. It was not until 1938, when Michael Macowan directed a production starring the notable Shakespearean actor Donald Wolfit, that *Volpone*'s fortunes changed radically for the better.

Performed at the Westminster Theatre, Macowan's production was the first public performance of *Volpone* on the London stage since the play came back into fashion. (The Phoenix Society's revival was a private event, and all other productions were in smaller cities.) In addition, Wolfit was the first theatrical luminary to take on the title role. Although actors in previous 20th-century productions delivered competent performances, none possessed the star power or charisma that Wolfit did. Thus, the London location and Wolfit's fame combined to make the 1938 production a landmark theatrical event. Cloaking Volpone in furs and attaching feathers to the legacy hunters, Macowan was the first modern director to emphasize the animal symbolism in the play. He even turned the *Avocatori*, characters not traditionally associated with an animal, into owl-like creatures. Macowan's choice to costume characters in a way that highlighted their bestial nature would be imitated by many directors in the ensuing decades. Other notable choices made by Macowan included his decision to excise the Would-be subplot and to use a gold-encrusted set for the action. Nearly every critic deemed Macowan's *Volpone* the best of the 20th-century revivals up to that point, and for the first time large numbers of people began to recognize how *Volpone* could sing on the stage.

Macowan's 1938 production was also significant because it served as a template for a slew of performances directed by, designed by and starring Wolfit in 1940, 1942, 1944, 1947, 1949 and 1953. Although Wolfit's revivals owed a debt to Macowan's production, each revival was noticeably different from both Macowan's staging and other earlier stagings by Wolfit. Wolfit's approach to the play was always evolving. The only constant was his approach to the character of Volpone. An agile, dynamic and even histrionic performer, Wolfit's talent and temperament were perfectly suited to the personality of Volpone. As Volpone, he exuded virility and an uncontrolled zeal for gold and women. He portrayed the fox as a highly sexual being who placed no limit on his many appetites. He also made Volpone the center of the play and moved all other characters to the periphery. As one of the last actor-managers, Wolfit treated his supporting cast as mere extras whose sole purpose was to serve his performance in the title role. This attitude led to a series of neutered Moscas. If there was a recurrent complaint about Wolfit's stagings, it was that he, unlike Macowan, denied Mosca any agency and relegated him to the status of meek servant.

As a director, Wolfit also experimented with various editorial approaches. In 1940 he reinserted the Would-bes into the text although Lady Would-be was played by a man in drag. In 1947 he removed Lady Would-be but retained Sir Pol and Peregrine, albeit in a much diminished capacity. Of all the editorial approaches taken to the Would-bes in the past century, this was perhaps the strangest and least successful. Over the years, Wolfit would also be criticized for his farcical approach to the play. Compared to Macowan's satirical treatment, Wolfit's over-the-top productions lacked subtlety and at times gravity. Nowhere was this more apparent than in his comedic staging of the trial. Despite these shortcomings, Wolfit's productions, perhaps because of his unequaled dynamism or perhaps because of their sheer frequency, became the definitive productions of *Volpone* in the 20th century. For those who were familiar with Wolfit's *Volpone*, it was impossible to direct a production that did not either consciously borrow or deviate from Wolfit's approach, especially when it came to the title character. Volpone belonged to Wolfit, much in the same way that Stanley Kowalski belonged to Marlon Brando. For decades to come, all future Volpones would be judged by their relationship to Wolfit's portrayal. In his 1976 essay 'Wolfit's Fox: An Interpretation of *Volpone*', R.B. Parker summed up the success, failure and undeniable significance of Wolfit's work:

> [The production] clearly had its limitations: the lack of ensemble playing, the often inferior supporting actors, the misplaced farce, the clumsy and increasingly tatty sets, the lack of splendour in properties and costumes. Yet, when all possible reservations have been made, Wolfit's interpretation remains the most exciting to date. This is because it expressed so brilliantly two basic truths about the play: the psychological essence of the protagonist, and the theatrical importance of his dimension as a performer. The core of Wolfit's fox was the 'pride of life' itself, a powerful and unrestrained libido which relishes life in all its sensual and energetic variety, including the black pleasures of cruelty and power. Such a Volpone becomes a surrogate for the audience's forbidden dreams. (p. 217)

In short, Wolfit was nothing less than an evangelist for Jonson's opus. Not only did his productions alter the trajectory of *Volpone* in the United Kingdom, they also changed how the play was perceived in North America. Wolfit's 1947 production was the first performance of *Volpone* on Broadway, and it sparked more than just a passing interest in the play. Because of Wolfit, *Volpone* became a play worthy of performance on both sides of the Atlantic; and in the following decades, it would go on to become the most produced Elizabethan or Jacobean play not written by William Shakespeare.

In the hands of the Titans: *Volpone* in the mid-20th century

In addition to Wolfit's frequent remounts, the 1940s saw two other professional productions of *Volpone*: a 1944 production at the Shakespeare Memorial Theatre at Stratford-upon-Avon and a 1948 production at the City Center of Music and Drama in New York City.

By nearly all accounts, both productions were uninspired and largely forgettable. Consequently, most theater historians consider the next production of note to be the 1952 production at the Shakespeare Memorial Theatre. Directed by George Devine and starring Ralph Richardson as Volpone and Anthony Quayle as Mosca, this production was perhaps best remembered for its lavish stage effects. Utilizing a wide variety of stage machinery, the performance included a re-creation of Venice's Grand Canal (replete with gondolas) and a golden bedchamber that disappeared beneath the stage at the end of the opening act. Despite being one of the leading actors of his generation, Richardson's performance received a combination of tepid praise and unequivocal condemnation. The most frequent charge leveled against Richardson was that his Volpone lacked passion. Compared to Wolfit's dynamic and wicked fox, Richardson's Volpone seemed listless and benign. The neutering of the play's central character also had the effect of taking the cynicism and cruelty out of Jonson's dark satire. Offsetting the weakness of Richardson was the strength of Quayle. Quayle's Mosca was unctuous and athletic, and for more than one reviewer, he called to mind a two-faced Puritan. In short, Devine's production inverted Wolfit's treatment of the Volpone-Mosca relationship. Whereas Wolfit's productions were consistently plagued by a passive parasite, the Memorial Theatre production suffered from a somnambulant magnifico, thus demonstrating the difficulty of finding the proper balance of power between master and servant.

Despite lacking a star such as Wolfit or Richardson, the 1955 naturalistic staging of *Volpone* by the Theatre Workshop made quite the splash. Representing Britain at the Paris International Theatre Festival, this production helped launch the career of Joan Littlewood, who would eventually come to be thought of as one of Britain's greatest 20th-century directors. Although Littlewood's *Volpone* did not have a charismatic actor in the title role, it more than made up for this deficiency with directorial invention and a stellar supporting cast. Littlewood was the first to modernize *Volpone*, finding 20th-century equivalents for the characters and costuming everyone in modern dress: Mosca smoked cigarettes, Corbaccio donned a beret, Sir Pol was weighted down by fishing and hunting gear and Celia wore a tight and revealing outfit. Even the props, which included a telephone and a cocktail shaker, were modern. All of this led an anonymous critic writing for *The Stage* to proclaim Littlewood's production 'the most excitingly alive production that London has seen for months' (quoted in Jensen, p. 65).

Following Littlewood's production, theatergoers would have to wait nine more years for another landmark production of *Volpone*. That production was Tyrone Guthrie's 1964 production at the Guthrie Theater in Minneapolis, Minnesota. Guthrie would direct *Volpone* twice, first at the theater bearing his name and again in 1968 at the National Theatre in London. The productions, both of which had sets and costumes designed by Tanya Moiseiwitsch, were quite similar in their approach. Both left Jonson's text largely intact although Guthrie did eliminate Volpone's epilogue from the National Theatre production in an attempt to highlight the cruelty of the *Avocatori*'s sentence. Both performances also failed to find a consistent tone. In his 1964 program notes, Guthrie proclaimed that 'there are no virtuous characters' in the play; however, the production's cynicism and borderline sadism was often contradicted by an over-the-top performance style that treated the play, especially the trial scenes, as a romp. This led to complaints from critics that Guthrie's staging of *Volpone* tried to do too many things and as a result ended up doing nothing. The most interesting aspect of Guthrie's production was his choice to literalize the characters' bestial traits: Volpone was cloaked in furs, Mosca buzzed like a fly and the trio of legacy hunters sported six-inch beaks and feathered capes. Even this choice, though, was greeted with ambivalence and frequently labeled excessive by reviewers. In his production history, R.B. Parker claimed that Guthrie's decision to equate the play's central characters with animals had the following consequence:

> The effect of so much invention was finally distracting, however, and the play's moral symbolism was undercut because, as Robert MacDonald complained in *The Scotsman*, 'it is difficult to condemn real vultures for behaving like vultures.' ('*Volpone* in Performance: 1921–1972', p. 152)

Thus, while highly inventive and visually engaging, Guthrie's efforts left most critics feeling dissatisfied.

In the late 1960s and early 1970s, *Volpone* reached the apex of its popularity with modern audiences. Some of the prominent theaters that presented *Volpone* during this period were South Coast Rep (California), Oregon Shakespeare Festival, Oxford Playhouse

(Oxford, England), New York Shakespeare Festival, Birmingham Rep (Birmingham, England), the Stratford Festival (Stratford, Canada) and the Bristol Old Vic (Bristol, England). At long last *Volpone* had become a frequent presence on the modern stage. The play also continued to attract some of the theater's biggest names. In 1977 Peter Hall directed a much-talked-about production for the National Theatre starring Paul Scofield as Volpone and Ben Kingsley as Mosca. In contrast to Guthrie's production nine years earlier, Hall's production was understated. The bestiary aspects of Jonson's text were completely ignored, and the characters were treated as real human beings as opposed to grotesque caricatures of people. The psychological realism of Hall's production, however, had the unfortunate consequence of undermining *Volpone*'s humor. It was almost as if Hall, perhaps in an effort to avoid the excessive levity and histrionics that plagued Guthrie's productions, overcompensated and took the playfulness out of the text. John Bury's minimalistic set was efficient and classy but arguably too ordered for the chaos of the play. Writing for the *Guardian*, Michael Billington described Bury's design as follows:

> John Bury has designed another elegant symmetrical set with a ceramic-tiled floor, folding doors that can change from beaten gold to bureaucratic white and a skeletal frame adumbrating the shape of St. Marks. But the new Hall-Bury style of lightweight classicism is a little too cool and precise for the tumultuous Jonsonian world. (27 April 1977)

The production's greatest strength was the ability of the actors, especially Scofield, to speak the verse quickly and intelligibly. Whereas many of Scofield's predecessors relied heavily on their physicality and agility in performance, Scofield used his prodigious vocal talents and the sheer power of Jonson's verse to create a stately Volpone. This verbal and languid approach to the title character also offered the perfect contrast to Kingsley's speedy urgency as an Iago-like Mosca. The distinct tempo-rhythms of the two men could not have been more complementary. The weak point of Hall's production, however, was the inconsistency of the supporting actors, who suffered from Hall's desire to present the characters as multidimensional and more complex than Jonson intended. Despite these shortcomings, Hall's production was undeniably the definitive production of the 1970s.

Volpone's popularity, especially in North America, tapered off in the 1980s. The most notable production from this decade was Bill Alexander's 1983 staging for the Royal Shakespeare Company. If nothing else, Alexander's uncut rendition of *Volpone* was remarkable for its length, lasting nearly four hours. Surprisingly, many appreciated the opportunity to see Jonson without editorial interference. The supporting cast, especially Miles Anderson as Mosca, was also well received. Richard Griffiths' performance in the title role produced a more ambivalent response among critics, though. A hefty actor prone to breathlessness and sweating, Griffiths lacked the athleticism that many other performers, most notably Wolfit, brought to the role. Consequently, he struggled to incarnate Volpone's zest for life and almost manic disposition. Instead, he came across as an actual invalid as opposed to a con artist impersonating an invalid. In short, Griffiths' avuncular portrayal was dismissed by several critics as lacking in force and inappropriate for the character. Alexander's staging concept, however, helped offset the problems created by the miscast Griffiths. Focusing on the importance of performance in the play, Alexander's production included a number of metatheatrical moments and devices, such as Volpone's frequent application of makeup and the use of a stage-within-a-stage. It should be noted that this directorial approach was also consistent with a mounting body of scholarship that was examining the role of performance and theatricality in *Volpone*.

Recent productions of *Volpone*

After a decline in the 1980s, *Volpone* experienced a mini-renaissance in the 1990s with major productions by the Almeida Theatre, the National Theatre and the Royal Shakespeare Company in England as well as by the Shakespeare Theatre Company in Washington, D.C. Fresh off the success of the megamusical *Miss Saigon*, Nicholas Hytner directed the Almeida's low-budget production of *Volpone* in 1990. Hytner's approach to the material was cynical and edgy with reviewers using adjectives such as 'punky', 'grotesque', 'venomous' and 'bleak' to describe the performance. To accentuate the play's darkness, he removed the Would-be subplot, which is more farcical and silly than the legacy hunting narrative. In addition, he took away any semblance of virtue in the play by transforming Celia into a feisty spitfire and Bonario into a dense, overgrown teenager. Perhaps influenced by a rise in queer studies in the 1980s and early 1990s, Hytner also highlighted the homoerotic aspects of Volpone's relationship with Mosca, going so far as to have Volpone undress Mosca while crying out, 'O, that I could now transform thee to a Venus!' The set design also had a bite to it, with Richard Allen Cave describing the concept as follows:

> Mark Thompson's design for a permanent setting for Nicholas Hytner's production of *Volpone* [featured a piled] mass of gilded objects (chiefly crates, chests, and trunks) on a stage flooded with water so that Volpone seemed enthroned in his bed on the heap of his ill-gotten gains which were slowly deliquescing into some Venetian canal. (p. 53)

Overall, Hytner's efforts were well received by critics who appreciated his fresh and sardonic take.

Making his directorial debut for the National Theatre in 1995, Matthew Warchus staged what was by far the most lavish and star-studded production in recent years. It featured Michael Gambon as Volpone and Simon Russell Beale as Mosca (along with a young Martin Freeman making his first professional stage appearance as 'third merchant'). The production, with sets and costumes designed by Richard Hudson, spared no expense. For this it was largely praised and occasionally derided. Among the extravagant costume pieces were a giant hearing aid for Corbaccio that critic Sarah Hemming compared to a periscope and hats for the *Avocatori* that ironically had the scales of justice balanced on top. The set was a labyrinth of corridors on a massive revolving stage. Cave gave this account of Hudson's design:

> Hudson manipulated the spatial vastness of the Olivier to his advantage by staging Matthew Warchus' production of *Volpone* on a revolving set that opened into a sequence of small, darkened rooms or confined exteriors which brought the play decidedly close to the audience; he achieved, too, a powerful overall symbol in that image of a revolving world within which the characters seemed to be trapped while racing for the spoils. ... There was always a sense that in that menacingly revolving edifice that the whirligig of time would soon bring in its revenges and that ... Volpone knew this on some deep psychological level, which

brought a chilling desperation and savagery to his scheming before time should run out on him. (pp. 52–3)

As for the acting, Gambon's work as Volpone was generally praised; however, quite a few critics noted that at times he struggled with his articulation, garbling and swallowing key lines of text. Russell Beale, on the other hand, received unqualified acclaim. Writing for the *Evening Standard*, Nick Curtis said the following about Russell Beale's work:

> Simon Russell Beale robs Gambon of much of the limelight. Mosca is a devastatingly prescient portrait of a Machiavellian meritocrat, a low-born man who, unlike his master, never lets his own cleverness blind him to the main chance. It's a masterpiece of timing that makes you long to see this heavyweight classical actor in more comic roles. (28 July 1995)

Guardian critic Michael Billington echoed these sentiments in his review:

> Simon Russell Beale, however, is the perfect Mosca: a man hooked on power as much as his master is on gold. Russell Beale shows someone for whom manipulation almost amounts to a sexual fetish.... [His words wing] across the stage like poison darts. (29 July 1995)

Like Hytner, Warchus also played up the homoeroticism in the play, spicing things up by having Volpone affectionately pet his parasite's codpiece. One last notable aspect of Warchus' production was his decision to open the play with a feverish dream sequence in which Volpone was chased by a fire-wielding mob. This foxhunt, which was broken by Volpone's first line, functioned as a nightmarish masque that framed the ensuing events. Although there were a few dissenters, Warchus' production was considered a triumph and earned the 28-year-old director an Olivier Award nomination for Best Director.

Although it did not receive nearly as much attention as the National Theatre's production, the 1996 production by Graeae Theatre Company, an English performance group committed to creating accessible yet cutting-edge work featuring performers with disabilities, was perhaps the most innovative staging of *Volpone* to date. Retitled *Flesh Fly*, Graeae's production utilized only six actors and a Sign Language interpreter who was also incorporated into the action. Despite the new title and some minor changes, *Flesh Fly* generally adhered to the words in Jonson's text; however, the casting radically altered the audience's experience of the play. A deaf actor (Neil Fox) played both Celia and Lady Would-be, thereby commenting on the ways in which women are silenced in the text. Jamie Beddard, an actor with cerebral palsy, performed the part of Corbaccio, making it much harder for an audience to laugh at Corbaccio's many ailments; and as a hypersexual Volpone, the legless yet kinetic Nabil Shaban wowed audiences by spending much of the play hanging upside down. In almost every moment, this vulgar and confrontational production challenged both Jonson's and audience members' assumptions about disease and disability. Director Ewan Marshall summed up his approach as follows:

> One of the play's main messages was that moral imperfection results in physical imperfection, such as Volpone's bastard offspring: the dwarf, the eunuch, and the hermaphrodite. This message is the complete opposite of what Graeae tries to communicate.... Having Nabil Shaban, who is a wheelchair user, playing Volpone allowed his physicality to add to the text by confusing and ultimately subverting Jonson's attempt to link moral and physical imperfection. (Giannachi and Luckhurst, pp. 62–3)

Thus, Graeae's radical staging offered a unique perspective on the play. By using disabled actors, the company was able to unearth new layers of meaning and change how audience members viewed both the text and disability.

The other notable production in 1996 was staged at the Shakespeare Theatre Company. Director Michael Kahn had seen Warchus' staging, and while he appreciated the acting, he thought that the production at the National Theatre neglected the comedic aspects of the play. Consequently, he made sure to bring a spirit of playfulness to his production the following year. The Shakespeare Theatre Company's production featured a number of humorous bells and whistles, including kazoos and a medical alert siren that Volpone deployed when the legacy hunters presented him with gifts. The most amusing addition made by Kahn was the transformation of the freaks' songs into big production numbers. Especially notable was Volpone's song of seduction, which was performed while Castrone and Androgyno danced Celia's clothes off. At times, however, Kahn's farcical approach led to laughter in unexpected and perhaps inappropriate places, such as Corvino's placing of a chastity belt on Celia and Volpone's return for the epilogue in prison apparel. The most revolutionary aspect of this production was Kahn's choice to cast Pat Carroll, a female comedian, as Volpone. Although the mustachioed Carroll was believable as a man, the decision to cross-cast the title role significantly affected the tone and trajectory of the production, for it took much of the menace and bite out of Volpone's misdeeds. Juxtaposed against Wallace Acton's effeminate Mosca, Carroll's Volpone did, however, make for an interesting study of gender ambiguity in the play. The set design was in keeping with the 17th-century Venetian location although it took a few liberties for the purpose of comic exaggeration. The costumes were a little less literal and paid tribute to the play's bestiary elements. Mosca sported antennae, and the legacy hunters' cloaks resembled bird tails. While more farcical than satirical, Kahn's production certainly accomplished his aim of inserting humor into the play.

One final production of note in the 1990s was the Royal Shakespeare Company's 1999 production directed by Lindsay Posner. The production starred Malcolm Storry as Volpone and Guy Henry as Mosca. Storry's Volpone was muscular and stolid. This characterization stood in stark contrast to Wolfit's excitable acrobat, Scofield's poised magnifico and Griffiths' corpulent invalid. Henry's Mosca came across as a supercilious, slimy worm that elicited comparisons to Shakespeare's Malvolio. Like Littlewood and Hall before him, Posner grounded the characters in realistic psychology. Although some comedy was inevitably lost, Posner, in contrast to Hall, did not completely negate the comedy in the play. He did this by combining realistic characterizations with a jovial tone that was reinforced with light music. The most frequently praised aspect of Posner's production was his striking use of color. The court scenes featured a rich scarlet while Volpone's makeup was a memorable green. Posner's production, though, will probably not be remembered as one of the seminal productions of the 20th century. Although the reviews on balance were more positive than negative, it was hardly the kind of production that inspired passionate enthusiasm.

Although the 21st century is still young, it seems as if interest in *Volpone* is dwindling slightly. In England this is probably no more than an inevitable slowing after a flurry of productions in the 1990s. Over a period of nine years, English audiences had the opportunity to see three of their finest theaters (the Almeida, the National and the Royal Shakespeare Company) mount major productions of *Volpone*, and if that was not sufficient for theatergoers, there were also smaller productions at the Lyric Theatre in Hammersmith (1991) and the Birmingham Repertory Theatre (1993). This glut of performances appears to have sated the English public's desire for additional productions of *Volpone*, and it also seems to have driven away directors who would rather resurrect more obscure classics. Paradoxically, *Volpone*'s previous success in England seems to be the cause of its present troubles. *Volpone*'s current struggles in America emanate from a different source. Unlike English audiences, American audiences have little affinity for Elizabethan or Jacobean playwrights not named Shakespeare. Put simply, it is incredibly difficult to make the economics of a Jonsonian production work in the United States; and without sizeable government subsidies, such as the ones available to companies in England, it has become increasingly rare for theaters in America to take the financial risk that comes with producing plays by Jonson. As a result, Americans saw only a handful of professional performances of *Volpone* during the closing years of the 20th century; and sadly, American productions of *Volpone* have become even scarcer in the 21st century.

Despite *Volpone*'s decline in popularity in the early 21st century, there have still been three notable productions: the 2004 production by the Royal Exchange Theatre in Manchester, the 2008 production by the American Shakespeare Center (ASC) in Virginia and the 2012 production by the Red Bull Theater in New York City. Although many critics dismissed the Royal Exchange Theatre's production as gimmicky and superficial, it did offer further proof of *Volpone*'s elasticity in performance. Director Greg Hersov went to great lengths to make his production accessible and relevant for modern audiences. He updated the language, adding terms such as VD and HIV. Hersov also excised most of the text belonging to Volpone's trio of freaks and transformed them into a dude, a nun and a nurse that resembled characters from the *Rocky Horror Picture Show*. As for the Sir Pol subplot, Hersov completely removed this from the play, claiming that the language was too topical for a contemporary audience to appreciate. In explaining his editorial approach, Hersov said:

> I was ruthless about cutting text that was difficult to understand and also rewrote the odd word to make the story clear. I think Jonson needs this. You must keep the audience with the action. Actually this leads to a very dynamic and exciting drive to the story without losing Jonson's subtlety and depth of perception. I think editing rigorously is essential for this play. (Personal Communication)

The cumulative effect of Hersov's cuts reduced *Volpone*, which routinely runs close to three hours, down to a manageable two and a half hours including intermission. In an effort to keep his audience engaged, Hersov also made music central to his production. Actors frequently wielded microphones as they sang an eclectic score featuring Italian pop songs and jazz numbers. Volpone's song of seduction to Celia even became a Barry White kind of number. Staged in the round, the Royal Exchange's production was also one of the more intimate productions of *Volpone*. The set was a modern metaphorical Venice that one reviewer compared to a Las Vegas hotel lounge. Hersov described the design concept as follows:

> The design was set in a fantasy Venice, a place through the ages associated with fantasy, beauty, death and decay. I'm sure Jonson, like Shakespeare, located Venice as a place of extravagant desires and corruption.... We had a three-level, fading white plaster surface eroded by water, on which we conjured up the various locales.... We concentrated on that Italian sharpness and elegance, so what money can get you was [attractively] shown to seduce the audience into the world of the play. (Personal Communication)

As for the acting, the physical antics of the performers impressed the critics, but it also muted the savagery of later scenes, such as the attempted rape of Celia and the trial sequence. In conclusion, Hersov's carnivalesque *Volpone* was not a production for the purists; however, it certainly offered a roadmap for those looking to update Jonson's 17th-century black comedy for a 21st-century audience.

In 2008 the American Shakespeare Center presented *Volpone* as part of its Actors' Renaissance Season. Perhaps even more interesting than the production was ASC's rehearsal process. ASC's goal is to produce English Renaissance drama using many of the practices common in the late 1500s and early 1600s. These practices include doubling actors, limiting the use of scenery and engaging directly with audience members. The Actors' Renaissance Season, which takes place every winter, goes a step further by requiring actors to rehearse in conditions similar to those in the Elizabethan and Jacobean eras. Productions have no director and limited rehearsal time. In addition, actors receive only their parts (i.e., their character's spoken text and the four cue words that precede those lines), thereby limiting their understanding of both narrative and character. As a result, actors in these productions tend to work very broadly, almost as if they were portraying stock characters. Furthermore, productions have no overarching aesthetic since there is not a director managing each aspect of the performance. Despite these limitations, the result can often be highly theatrical and engaging. ASC staged *Volpone* as a comedy. This unwavering commitment to the play's humor held true even in the rape scene, which was staged like a cartoonish vaudeville skit with Volpone galloping around in his underwear trying futilely to pry Celia's legs apart. Much of the humor in the production also derived from the pace at which the play was performed. John Harrell, the actor who portrayed Volpone, described his approach to performing Jonson in the following way:

> I think that an actor serves Jonson best by cracking his lines off almost faster than an audience can absorb them, and for the con men, certainly faster than any of the marks can react to them. ... I find performing Jonson in this way to be exhilarating, nearly improvisatory, and satisfactorily physical. (Bessell, p. 102)

In a production with limited set pieces and therefore no transitions between scenes, this approach to speaking the text gave the sensation of constant motion. Thus, by stripping away all the bells and whistles associated with the modern theater and speeding up the actors' delivery, ASC was able to tap into the frenzy at the heart of *Volpone*.

Other than ASC's 2008 staging, there was not a major professional performance of *Volpone* in America between the 1996 production by the Shakespeare Theatre Company and the 2012 production by the Red Bull Theater. The Red Bull Theater production, however, could not have been timelier. The production's director, Jesse Berger, described *Volpone*'s relevance as follows:

> The deeper we got into stories of Bernie Madoff and the economic 'bad actors,' [the more] we realized *Volpone* would fit with our time and would examine the role of money in our culture and its corrupting influence. ('Production Notebook: Red Bull Theater's *Volpone*', p. 34)

In addition, the overwhelmingly positive reception of the Red Bull production proved that American audiences could still appreciate Jonson's comedy. Featuring stage stalwarts Stephen Spinella (Volpone), Tovah Feldshuh (Lady Would-be) and Alvin Epstein (Corbaccio), the production boasted uniformly excellent acting that balanced truthfulness with comic exaggeration. Berger also cut the text in a highly intelligent way, preserving Lady Would-be and the freaks while discarding Sir Pol and Peregrine. To cut down his cast size, Berger also transformed the four *Avocatori* into one *Avocatore*. Collectively, these edits produced a lean performance text that still retained the essential strengths and character of Jonson's original. The most exciting aspect of Berger's production, though, was the steampunk design concept. The set featured arty yet simple Venetian backdrops while the costuming and makeup merged Elizabethan and punk sensibilities with a nod to the play's bestiary elements. Wig and hair designer, Charles LaPointe, offered these thoughts on the design scheme:

> The Elizabethans inspired everything in this show, but all you had to do was twist the hair a certain way, throw in a funky color and you change the whole feel of it. It's meant to look weird and off-kilter. For example, Castrone is dressed like an Elizabethan, but he's got straps around his body referencing steampunk. ('Production Notebook: Red Bull Theater's *Volpone*', p. 35)

And costume designer Clint Ramos added the following:

> The aesthetic we were shooting for was Elizabethan with a bit of punk and grunge. We kept it in this black world, and we operated on imageries of birds.... I wanted characters like Nano and Castrone, who entertain Volpone, to manifest the same decay as Volpone but in a punk, rock-and-roll kind of way, with some sexuality and androgyny. So we went into Vivienne Westwood and punk London to give the sense that they lived

in dungeons and just popped up when called for. ('Production Notebook: Red Bull Theater's *Volpone*', p. 34)

In short, Red Bull's production managed to be simultaneously modern and faithful to the spirit of Jonson's 1606 text. It was quite the accomplishment, and for this it was warmly received by both critics and patrons hungering for a chance to see a play that is all too rarely performed in the United States.

Where *Volpone* will go next is impossible to predict. Although England seems certain to eventually emerge from its mild *Volpone* fatigue, the play's commercial prospects in the United States remain dicey. It seems unlikely that the play will have three different professional productions a year, as sometimes happened during the 1960s and 1970s; however, the positive view that both artists and scholars continue to have of the text should also prevent *Volpone* from descending into complete obscurity, as it did in the 19th century. The play undeniably still works in performance, and there are many staging possibilities that have yet to be seen. Although *Volpone* will probably be performed with a little less frequency in the 21st century, the productions should be no less exciting.

5 The Play on Screen

Traditional versions of *Volpone* on screen

Until recently there was not a readily available film that used Jonson's text. This changed in 2010 when Stage on Screen, a company dedicated to producing DVDs of classic plays, recorded a live staging of *Volpone* at the Greenwich Theatre in London. Before the Stage on Screen version, the only recording that garnered any attention was a 1959 version that Donald Wolfit made as part of BBC's *World Theatre* series. According to Ejner Jensen, who extensively researched *Volpone*'s stage and screen history, the BBC destroyed all copies of this film in their archives; however, R.B. Parker, who conducted his research prior to Jensen, was able to view Wolfit's work and thought the following:

> It is only a ghost of Wolfit's stage portrayal. Without the audience response which fed his energy, with his vocal power muted for the microphones, with sexual innuendo cut in the interests of family viewing, and with [director Stephen Harrison's] stolid camera angles, the interpretation loses size, fluidity, and bite. Despite diminished excitement, however, it can still give a useful sense of Wolfit's interpretation. ('Wolfit's Fox: An Interpretation of *Volpone*', p. 201)

In addition to their 1959 version, the BBC also recorded *Volpone* in 1948 and 1965, and in 1969 the CBC aired a heavily cut version of the play. Regrettably, none of these made-for-television films is publicly distributed.

The Stage on Screen production is a faithful but modern rendering of Jonson's play. Directed by Elizabeth Freestone, this recorded live performance contains only small edits to Jonson's script, the most prominent of which is the excision of Volpone's song of seduction to Celia. Although it preserves most of Jonson's text, the production does still feature modern clothing and props. Costume pieces such as Volpone's cream three-piece suit and Corvino's snazzy brown pinstripe suit add style and sophistication. Consisting of a bed, a moveable platform, a black-and-white tile floor and little else, the minimalistic set reinforces the elegant costuming. Stage makeup is also used effectively. A heavily sunburned Politic Would-be elicits laughter, and Mosca is so pallid that he resembles a member of the Addams Family. Although the film is not laugh-out-loud funny, it consistently amuses with its sardonic edge. Freestone's cynical humor is most apparent in her treatment of Celia and Bonario. Speaking in a heavy Irish brogue, Celia obnoxiously boohoos as she struggles with a chastity belt; and in a gesture of comic ridiculousness, Bonario offers an ice cream cone to a 'disconsolate' Mosca during their Act III scene. One final example of Freestone's cynicism is her decision to double-cast the freaks as the *Avocatori*. It is these little directorial inventions throughout that bring a wry quality to the film. The film is also well paced with actors speaking quickly and conversationally. Very seldom does one feel as if s/he is listening to a verse drama. Thus, the manner of speech adds yet another hint of the contemporary to the performance. If there is a criticism to be made of the film, it is that the acting, especially Richard Bremmer's work in the title role, is too understated. As with other productions that emphasize psychological realism, the mania and zaniness of the characters is too often lost or muted in the film of Freestone's production. Nevertheless, after many years without an available recording of *Volpone*, the Stage on Screen rendition is a welcome resource for scholars, students and lovers of Jonson's comic masterpiece.

Translations and adaptations of *Volpone* on screen

Volpone's life on film consists mostly of adaptations. Beginning with Maurice Tourneur's *Volpone* in 1941, there have been four notable cinematic adaptations: Tourneur's, Joseph Mankiewicz's *The Honey Pot* (1967), Maurizio Ponzi's *Il Volpone* (1988) and Frédéric Auburtin's *Volpone* (2003). Of these four films, only *The Honey Pot* is in English. Since none of the foreign language films provides English subtitles, monolingual viewers may have difficulty following the narrative at certain points; however, all of these films make use of Jonson's characters and premise, which is incredibly helpful to anyone familiar with Jonson's play. Despite their debt to Jonson, these films are also undeniably original works that treat Jonson's play as source material for a new creative endeavor. (Those interested in adaptations for other media may want to explore George Antheil's opera *Volpone*, Thomas Sterling's novel *The Evil of the Day*, the Broadway musical *Foxy* and Larry Gelbart's farce *Sly Fox*.) By viewing these films, one can gain insight into how modern artists are able to adapt a 17th-century stage play for a new medium and audience.

It is impossible to speak about Tourneur's 1941 film without first mentioning Stefan Zweig's 1926 adaptation of *Volpone* for the German stage. Zweig's adaptation was wildly successful both in Europe, where it continues to be performed, and in the United States, where it outshone Jonson's original in the 1920s and 30s. Zweig's adaptation makes the following alterations to Jonson's text:

1. It removes the Sir Pol subplot and Volpone's freaks.
2. It deletes the Scoto of Mantua sequence.
3. It adds a prostitute named Canina who seeks Volpone's hand in marriage.
4. It changes the names of Bonario and Celia to Leone (the lion) and Colomba (the dove). These name changes also hint at a change in characterization: Leone is a boisterous and volatile sea captain, and Colomba is pure to the point of imbecility.
5. It reduces Volpone's motivations to greed and cruelty, eliminating the ennui and artistry that drive him in Jonson's text.
6. It transforms Mosca from a sadistic villain into a populist hero.
7. It modifies the ending so that Mosca ends up with Volpone's wealth, which he then redistributes to the cheated legacy hunters and the people of Venice.
8. Tonally, it shifts the work from disturbing satire to gleeful farce.

Two years after his German adaptation, Zweig gave the French writer Jules Romains permission to work on a modified version to suit the tastes of French theatergoers. For the most part, Romains translated Zweig's text; however, he went even further than Zweig in purging the play of its dark character, doing everything possible to reduce the sadistic behavior and graphic language in the script. Romains then revisited *Volpone* a decade later when he authored the screenplay for Tourneur's film. The biggest difference between the Zweig-Romains stage version and the screenplay authored by Romains is the addition of a 20-minute prologue. Through the movie's opening sequence, the audience learns that Volpone is a merchant with two ships at sea and that his fellow merchant, Corvino, has financed this venture. When Corvino, with Voltore acting as his lawyer, comes to collect his debt, Volpone turns to the moneylender Corbaccio for additional funds. Disaster strikes when one of Volpone's ships goes missing. He is thrown in jail because he cannot pay his debts, and it is in jail that he first encounters Mosca. When Volpone's missing ship and the precious cargo surprisingly reappear, Volpone is released. He then bails out his new friend Mosca, and the two devise a scheme for exacting revenge against those responsible for Volpone's imprisonment. The effect of the prologue is twofold: it contextualizes and perhaps justifies Volpone's plot to con the legacy hunters, and it gives a complete history of the relationship between Volpone and Mosca. Once Volpone and Mosca are out of jail, the remainder of the film follows the general arc of the Zweig-Romains stage adaptation; however, Mosca's distribution of wealth to the masses at the end of the film has a Marxist slant that is more muted in the stage version. In comparing Tourneur's film to Jonson's play, James Welsh offers this unflattering assessment:

> There can be no doubt that the play *Volpone* has been violated, foreshortened, and diluted both in structure and effect. Although the predatory characters of Jonson's original are generally preserved and recognizable, the relationship between Volpone and Mosca is seriously changed, and their dispositions at the end of the play Jonson himself would probably not recognize. The resemblance of this film to the play from which it ultimately derives is mainly situational, and the adaptation is very loose indeed. (p. 43)

Perhaps the greatest strength of this black-and-white film is the acting, which features theatrical gestures and comically exaggerated facial expressions. With the exception of Louis Jouvet, who plays a buttoned-up and conspiratorial Mosca, nothing about the performances is subtle. This over-the-top approach does much to enhance the comedy. Especially noteworthy is Charles Dullin as the nasally Corbaccio. Unfortunately, Tourneur's *Volpone* is marred by anti-Semitism and the long shadow cast by the Nazi occupation of France. The Jewish Zweig is absent from the credits; and although he is referred to as a 'Levantine', the character of Volpone is clearly coded as Jewish. This has prompted more than one critic to note the similarities between the Volpone of Tourneur's film and 20th-century representations of Shakespeare's villainous Shylock. In addition, the actor playing Volpone, Harry Baur, was known for his portrayal of Jewish characters. In fact, he played so many Jewish characters that in 1943 the Nazis mistook him for a Jew, and he died as a result of injuries suffered at the hands of the Gestapo. Despite the problems with the screenplay and the implicit stereotypes in Tourneur's film, many still consider *Volpone* to be the greatest film of an early master filmmaker; and even today it remains the most widely viewed and discussed cinematic adaptation of *Volpone*.

Based on a play (*Mr. Fox of Venice* by Frederick Knott) that was based on a novel (*The Evil of the Day* by Thomas Sterling) that was in turn based on Jonson's *Volpone*, *The Honey Pot* is the final product of an elaborate game of 'Telephone' played by various artists across different centuries and media. Written and directed by Hollywood legend Joseph Mankiewicz, *The Honey Pot* is a lighthearted murder mystery that stars Rex Harrison, Maggie Smith and Cliff Robertson. Stylistically, *The Honey Pot* is a strange blend of Noël Coward's society comedies and Agatha Christie's parlor mysteries. The film is set in the lavish Venetian *palazzo* of the eccentric millionaire Cecil Fox (Harrison). Fox has hired William McFly (Robertson) to assist him in a 'practical joke' that he wants to play on three former mistresses. Fox's plan is to lure these women to his residence under the pretense that he is dying and searching for an heir. He then pits the women against each other, extorting both gifts and sexual favors from them. His joke, however, is far more sinister than it first appears, and the film morphs into a whodunit when one of the legacy hunters, a millionairess from Texas named Mrs. Lone Star Crockett Sheridan, dies from a suspicious drug overdose. Her nurse, Sarah Watkins (Smith), then transforms into an amateur sleuth and helps expose the perpetrator of this nefarious deed. At the climax of the film, it is revealed that Fox, who is Sheridan's common-law husband, is destitute and that he orchestrated the murder in an attempt to inherit Sheridan's fortune. Once exposed, Fox takes his own life. With the mystery solved, the film concludes with McFly and Watkins gallivanting through St. Mark's Square as the deceased Fox and Sheridan can be heard bickering from the Great Beyond. This ending brings a touch of romance to the film and mitigates the gloomy finality of the earlier deaths. While amusing and suspenseful, the plot of *The Honey Pot* defies logic at times, and there are several instances where characters behave in ways that explicitly contradict their nature; nevertheless, the film, through its shrewd manipulation of the source material, manages to keep viewers on their toes. The relationship between the film and the play is immediately apparent, as *The Honey Pot* begins with Fox watching a private performance of Act V of *Volpone*. And throughout the film there are frequent allusions to both Jonson and his play. Some of these allusions, such as Fox's whiskey coming from a town called Jonson, are merely for the enjoyment of the observant viewer. However, there are others that play a more prominent role. Pascale Aebischer describes the relationship between play and film in the following terms:

> There is ample evidence that Jonson's play is the principal pre-text and intertext of this clever comedy of manners that ends up being a murder mystery. Characters consciously insert themselves in the Jonsonian plot to the extent that they cite the Act in which they believe they have arrived, fight against their positions within the plot and adapt it to suit their own needs.... It is a perfect example of the ways in which early modern pre-texts have prompted even the most mainstream directors to explore the boundaries of their medium and produce adaptations that use the early modern past to prove the vices of the present. (p. 152)

Thus, from the beginning Mankiewicz prepares his audience for the fact that *The Honey Pot* will consciously deviate from the plot of Jonson's play. This, in turn, builds suspense and causes viewers to guess at how Mankiewicz's characters may fare compared to Jonson's characters. Mankiewicz also capitalizes on the audience's mistaken assumption that McFly, like Mosca, is devious and will eventually double-cross his employer. Just as Mosca surprises the audience in Act V of *Volpone* with his duplicity, McFly stuns *The Honey Pot*'s audience with his honesty. Throughout the film McFly's behavior appears suspect, so the revelation that Fox is the real and lone villain is quite the *coup de théâtre*. It is this persistent and surprising interplay between the two works that is *The Honey Pot*'s greatest strength.

Although it lacks the star power of other cinematic adaptations of *Volpone*, Maurizio Ponzi's 1988 film *Il Volpone* still makes for interesting viewing. Like *The Honey Pot*, *Il Volpone* is set in the present day; however, it is not located in Venice but in the scenic Ligurian Riviera. In Ponzi's film Ugo Maria Volpone is the owner of a shipping company, and Bartolomeo Mosca is his new valet. Assisted and at times egged on by their wives, Volpone's three friends – Raffaele Voltore, Ernesto Corbaccio and Ciro Corvino – aim to win his fortune. A shipping tycoon like Volpone, Voltore parts with his most important vessel. Corbaccio, a car dealer, gives Volpone his prized Maserati; and Corvino offers a night with his wife Francesca, the town's attractive young mayor. Volpone gleefully takes all of these, and for his final trick he fakes his own death in a Maserati accident. He then retreats to his bunker where he watches the reading of the will through a security camera. After Mosca is declared Volpone's heir and the legacy hunters depart in despair, Volpone asks Mosca to release him from his bunker; instead, Mosca disconnects the security camera while Volpone discovers that he has been locked in. The film ends with Volpone playing solitaire in the bunker while the devious Mosca feasts and plays poker upstairs with a group of servants who intentionally let him win. This scene is a reprise of the film's opening when the legacy hunters throw their poker game with Volpone, and in the film's final image it is clear that Mosca grasps that he, like his former master, will now be hunted for his wealth. This conclusion suggests that the characters are doomed to a perpetual game of 'King of the Mountain'. Mosca has dethroned Volpone, but in doing so he has laid the groundwork for his future demise. Thus, his coup is more of a Pyrrhic victory than the unequivocal triumph by Tourneur's Mosca and Mankiewicz's McFly; nevertheless, it is still a far more favorable outcome than the whipping that Jonson's Mosca suffers, and as a result, it challenges Jonson's assertion that virtue is rewarded and vice is punished. In addition to Ponzi's reworking of the ending, the other interesting innovation in the film is the decision to make Corvino's wife a reluctant yet willing participant in sexual congress with Volpone. By eliminating sexual assault from the narrative, Ponzi makes it much easier for the viewer to sympathize with Volpone, and he makes Francesca a far more compelling and psychologically complex character than Celia. These changes, coupled with the film's modern feel, help make *Il Volpone* unpredictable and relatable.

Written by Eric-Emmanuel Schmitt and directed by Frédéric Auburtin, the 2003 *Volpone* is a 90-minute romp that aired as a Christmas movie on French television. The film stars Gérard Depardieu, one of the world's most famous character actors, and it is clearly written to showcase his comedic gifts. Set in the 15th century, the film opens with Volpone, Nano and Castrato fleeing the authorities in Tuscany. (This is the only cinematic adaptation that retains Volpone's freaks although they are reduced from a trio to a duo and Castrone is renamed.) After eluding his pursuers, Volpone encounters Mosca peddling junk medicine in a tavern. When Mosca is arrested, Volpone helps him escape. The two then head for Naples, and it is there that they begin their scheme. Like Jonson's *Volpone*, the film features three legacy hunters: Grappione, Secco and Corbaccio. (It should be noted that Secco is patterned after Jonson's Corbaccio while the Corbaccio in the film is much closer to Jonson's Corvino.) For the most part, the con proceeds as it does in Jonson's play; however, there are two major differences between Jonson's play and Schmitt's screenplay. The first is the addition of Volpone's fictitious brother Balduccio, whom Volpone pretends to be whenever he wishes to shed the guise of an invalid and satisfy his appetites in the city. The second is Schmitt's decision to make Celia, who is married to Corbaccio, a willing accomplice of Volpone and Mosca. Although Mosca and Volpone still have a falling out, the film concludes with their reconciliation as they flee the authorities with Celia. Sarah Hatchuel and Nathalie Vienne-Guerrin make the following observation about the film's denouement:

> As in Jonson's play, the villains are chased and 'punished by the laws', but they eventually escape and the spectators laugh with them at the thought of their lively, albeit immoral, future. In this version, 'mischiefs' do not 'bleed' when they are 'fat' but are rather destined to prosper again. (p. 514)

Thus, the 2003 film of *Volpone* dramatizes a cycle in which Volpone and Mosca deceive, get exposed and escape so that they can deceive again. It is a fun ride and one that fittingly concludes with the image of the con artists galloping off together in a carriage.

Although there are many differences between these four adaptations, it is their similarities that are most striking. All of these adaptations eliminate Sir Pol, Lady Would-be and any evidence of the play's

Britishness. They also make significant modifications to the characters' motivations, often going so far as to transform Mosca from villain into hero. In addition, they are all concerned with the origin of the Volpone-Mosca relationship. Most notably, these films eschew Jonson's catastrophe in which everyone suffers defeat, and they replace it with something more befitting a traditional comedy. For Tourneur, Mankiewicz and Ponzi, the new ending is the triumph of the fly. For Auburtin it is the mutual triumph of Volpone and Mosca. This is not to say that these films are Pollyannaish in their approach; but noticeably absent is the harsh and brutal judgment of the court. This change blunts Jonson's didacticism and replaces it with something more upbeat. Thus, these cinematic adaptations adopt only half of Horace's important maxim: they delight but do not teach. Whether this constitutes an improvement upon or a diminishment of Jonson's play remains a matter of great contention.

6 Critical Assessments

When writing critical literature, scholars typically argue about a work's quality or its meaning. Critics who defend or attack the artistic merit of a particular work are participating in critical valuation while those who try to decipher a work's meaning are engaging in critical interpretation. Both aspects of criticism have implications that extend far beyond the confines of universities and classrooms. The critical reception of a play can determine whether or not it continues to be produced while the critical interpretation of a play can shape how it is staged. This is certainly true of *Volpone*, and it is my hope that the connection between the critical history detailed in this chapter and the performance history discussed earlier in the book will be readily apparent.

Critical valuation

The critical fortunes of *Volpone* have fluctuated wildly in the centuries following its 1607 publication. Although a little simplistic, the general arc of *Volpone*'s critical reception can be summarized as follows: *Volpone* is exceptionally popular and greatly esteemed in its time and throughout the 17th century. As Neoclassicism gives way to Sentimentalism and Romanticism during the latter part of the 18th century, critical opinion of *Volpone* and Jonson declines significantly. Modernism's triumph over Romanticism in the late 19th and early 20th century fosters a reappraisal and rediscovery of *Volpone*. Now in the era of Postmodernism, *Volpone*'s place in the canon is again secure, and this has allowed critics to appreciate the play without glossing over its imperfections.

Any discussion of the critical literature surrounding *Volpone* must begin with the first commentary on the play: the prologue and the

Epistle in the 1607 Quarto. Until the 20th century, when authorial intent ceases to be a matter of cardinal importance, Jonson's prolix treatise and statement of purpose serve as the lens through which nearly all critics evaluate *Volpone*. In the age of Neoclassicism, the play is praised to the extent that it adheres to the artistic principles outlined in the prologue and Epistle, and in the Romantic era the play is rejected largely because of the artistic principles stated in the prologue and Epistle; however, these texts are canards that throw critics and readers off the scent. After encountering Jonson's opinion of the play, the reader no longer sees *Volpone* for what it is; instead, s/he sees it for what the prologue and Epistle say it is: a traditional, highly structured work with a clear moral message. It is only in the past century, after the advent of New Criticism, that scholars have been able to approach the play without the bias and baggage engendered by the prologue and Epistle. The result is a valuation of the play based upon its complexity and relevance as opposed to its use of and adherence to a certain set of rules fashionable in the 17th century.

Perhaps the most important remark in either of Jonson's prefatory materials is this seemingly innocuous rhyming couplet in the prologue: 'The laws of Time, Place, Persons he observeth,/From no needful rule he swerveth' (ll. 31–2). By touting his adherence to the traditional principles of playwriting, Jonson sets the standard by which others will judge and evaluate his work; but what are these laws and needful rules that Jonson alludes to, and how do they shape the early critical appraisal of *Volpone*? In short, they are the basic tenets of Neoclassicism and can be enumerated as follows:

1. Unity of Time – The dictum that the entirety of a play's action must occur within a 24-hour period.
2. Unity of Place – The dictum that the entirety of a play's action must occur in one location. In the strictest sense, this means one house. In the broader sense, it means the play must be situated in the same city. It is the broader understanding of this rule that Jonson uses in *Volpone*.
3. Unity of Persons – The dictum that a character's behavior must be internally consistent as well as consistent with his/her position in society.
4. Unity of Action – The dictum that a play must have one central action from which all events spring. This rule prohibits the use of

subplots and leads to the censure of plot points that are not the logical consequence of previously dramatized events.
5. The Principle of Verisimilitude – The dictum that all events in the play must be plausible.
6. The Rewarding of Good and the Punishing of Evil – The dictum that all unsavory characters and actions receive an appropriate punishment.
7. Purity of Genres – The dictum that a play must not mix tragedy and comedy.

Regarding the laws of time and place, *Volpone* is undeniably in compliance. The play also clearly rewards good and punishes evil although the source of that judgment is dubious at best. Even though the play's ending is decidedly uncomic, critics in the 17th and 18th centuries seldom attack Jonson for violating the purity of genres. They refrain from doing so primarily because Jonson's Epistle does such a stellar job of defending the play's ending as necessary for the punishing of evil and the imparting of a moral lesson. Thus, we are left with three 'needful rules' (unity of persons, unity of action and the principle of verisimilitude) for early critics to focus upon. For critics writing in the 17th and 18th centuries, Jonson's violation of these core principles is a black mark on *Volpone*, and it diminishes their estimation of the work.

When citing Jonson's violation of the unity of persons, early critics focus primarily on the figure of Volpone. In particular, they argue that his decision to taunt the legacy hunters in Act V after so narrowly escaping danger in Act IV is out of character. This charge is leveled by multiple critics and is best summed up by the dramatist John Dennis in 1696:

> The Character of Volpone is Inconsistent with it self [sic]. ... The Inconsistence of the Character appears in this, that Volpone in the fifth Act behaves himself like a Giddy Coxcombe, in the Conduct of that very Affair which he manag'd so craftily in the first four. ... The design of Volpone is to Cheat, he has carried on a Cheat for three years together, with Cunning and with Success. And yet he on a sudden in cold blood does a thing, which he cannot but know must Endanger the ruining all. (quoted in Craig, p. 343)

In addition to those who claim Volpone's behavior is internally inconsistent, there are also individuals who argue that Jonson's characterization of the *Avocatori* does not match their position in society. In the neoclassical theater kings are expected to behave like kings, servants like servants and judges like judges. The corruption of the court and the *Avocatori*'s shameless pandering to Mosca, however, violate traditional expectations about how officers of the law should behave. Giving voice to this complaint is Richard Cumberland, who states that Jonson 'has made a wanton breach of character and gained but a sorry jest by the bargain, when he violates the dignity of his court of judges by making one of them so abject in his flattery to the Parasite' (quoted in Barish, p. 42). Over the ensuing centuries these claims and their like have been summarily dismissed; however, one cannot discount their importance in shaping *Volpone*'s early critical valuation.

Critics who find the play's action to be lacking in unity focus on two areas: the Sir Pol subplot and the events of the play's final act. In addition to affecting the estimation of *Volpone*'s literary merit, attacks on the Sir Pol episodes also result in the eradication of the subplot from late 18th-century productions. John Dennis asserts that Sir Pol and Peregrine should 'be look'd upon as Excrescencies' (quoted in Craig, p. 343). And in an even harsher criticism, Peter Whalley writes:

> This whole episode of Sir Politick [sic] Would-be never did, nor ever can please. He seems to be brought in merely to lengthen out the play. ... I cannot help thinking this episode to be rather an excrescence than a beauty, as it has no sort of connection with the rest of the play. (quoted in Barish, pp. 34–5)

As for the accusation that *Volpone*'s final act represents a departure from the play's earlier events, it is a charge oft repeated in the 17th and 18th centuries. The clearest and most temperate version of this critique comes from the prominent poet, playwright and critic John Dryden. He writes:

> The unity of design seems not exactly observed in [*Volpone*]; for there appear two actions in the play; the first naturally ending with the fourth act; the second forced from it in the fifth: which yet is the less to be condemned in him, because the disguise of Volpone, though it suited not with his character as a crafty or covetous person, agreed well enough with that of

a voluptuary; and by it the poet gained the end he aimed at, the punishment of vice, and the reward of virtue, which that disguise produced. So that to judge equally of it, it was an excellent fifth act, but not so naturally proceeding from the former. (quoted in Barish, p. 28)

The problem of the play's double climax is one that still vexes. Although most modern critics have found a way to weave Act V successfully into the fabric of the play, productions still struggle to acquire momentum in the play's final act, perhaps proving that there is some merit to Dryden's observation.

Most who object to the plausibility of *Volpone* claim that the play's events could not reasonably occur within a 24-hour period. In many ways this judgment resembles the controversy surrounding Corneille's *The Cid*. Like *The Cid*, *Volpone* is censured because its adherence to the unity of time makes the volume of incidents in the play improbable. Although she uses Jonson's violation of verisimilitude to justify her own such breach, Margaret Cavendish, a writer and wife of one of Jonson's patrons, still offers the best summary of Jonson's offense. She notes:

Ben Johnson [sic] as I have heard was of that opinion, that a comedy cannot be good, nor is a natural or true Comedy, if it should present more than one dayes [sic] action, yet his Comedies that he hath published, could never be the actions of one day; for could any rational person think that the whole Play of the Fox could be the action of one day? (quoted in Craig, p. 234)

Modern critics have since come to realize that Jonson's aim is not plausibility, but in the age of Neoclassicism, when the assumption is that the playwright should always strive for verisimilitude, Jonson is taken to task for failing to craft a plausible plot.

Despite this list of quibbles, the general consensus about *Volpone* during the 1600s and the first half of the 1700s is that it is a work of extraordinary genius. Even those who find fault with some aspect of the play still declare it largely worthy of praise. Cavendish includes *Volpone* in her list of Jonson's masterpieces and praises its wit and careful construction. Dryden sees virtue in *Volpone*'s continuity of scenes while Dennis concedes that he admires 'the strength of Ben Johnson's [sic] Judgment' (quoted in Craig, p. 342). Further proof of *Volpone*'s critical acceptance comes from its repeated citation in the

1655 *English Treasury of Wit and Language*. Richard Hurd says about the play that it 'is a subject so manifestly fitted for all times, that it stands in need of no vindication' (quoted in Barish, p. 34); and Richard Cumberland remarks:

> After all it will be confessed that the production of such a drama as *The Fox* in the space of five weeks is a very wonderful performance; for it must on all hands be considered as the master-piece of a very capital artist, a work, that bears the stamp of elaborate design, a strong and frequently sublime vein of poetry, much sterling wit, comic humour, happy character, moral satire and unrivalled erudition. (quoted in Barish, p. 39)

Sadly, Cumberland's enthusiastic praise in 1788 is the last the play will receive for approximately a century.

The critical valuation of *Volpone* begins to shift during the second half of the 18th century. This change in fortune is the result of the ascendance of two new artistic philosophies: Sentimentalism and Romanticism. The decline in critical opinion is gradual and is initially seen in performance reviews, such as this 1771 anonymous review of a production at Covent Garden, that hold the play up as good literature but bad theatre:

> But, with all these perfections, [*Volpone*] seems better calculated to afford pleasure in the Closet, than on the Stage, as there is an evident deficiency of incident, and interest in the Catastrophe, which renders it incapable of giving that satisfaction in the Representation, it undoubtedly must afford on a perusal. (quoted in Barish, p. 36)

In 1800 Charles Dibdin repeats this opinion in *A Complete History of the English Stage*:

> *Volpone; or the Fox*, was performed in 1605, and has been generally considered as Jonson's best production. Certainly the plot is upon a very meritorious principle, and the characters are forcibly drawn.... The group of characters that are introduced to work up those materials, are full of contrast, strength, and nature; would not one think it, therefore, very extraordinary that this piece, even supported by admirable acting, has never greatly succeeded? Nothing, considered superficially, can be so unaccountable; but, when the subject is fairly investigated, nothing can be more clearly comprehended. Quaint, dry, studied correctness,

unsupported by quickness, spirit, and fire, can never satisfy. The author in this piece conducts us into a uniform and proportionable building, presents us with an entertainment, and introduces us to company, but the apartments are cheerless vaults, the viands are carved marble, and the guests are statues. (quoted in Barish, pp. 43–4)

In short, *Volpone* goes from being condemned by the overly academic neoclassical critics for not being fully uniform and proportional to being condemned by Romantic critics who abhor any vestige of 'studied correctness' in works of art.

Volpone's status plummets further in the 19th century when its literary merit comes under fire as well. Leading the assault are the famed literary critic William Hazlitt and the great poet Samuel Taylor Coleridge. Hazlitt writes:

[Jonson's] plots are improbable by an excess of consistency.... The whole is worked up too mechanically, and our credulity overstretched at last revolts into scepticism, and our attention overtasked flags into drowsiness. This play seems formed on the model of Plautus, in unity of plot and interest; and old Ben, in emulating his classic model, appears to have done his best. There is the same caustic unsparing severity in it as in his other works. His patience is tried to the utmost. His words drop gall. (quoted in Barish, pp. 49–50)

Thus, Hazlitt continues Dibdin's attack on *Volpone* by focusing on its surgical construction. In the age of Romanticism, emotion displaces reason while intuitive creativity supplants studied precision. This is why the Romantics are the first to hold Shakespeare up as the model playwright. His plays are sprawling and uncontrolled, a tour de force of poetic imagination. Jonson, in contrast, is emblematic of the academy and an antiquated approach to playwriting. It does not matter that *Volpone* is, in its own way, an antiestablishment work. The only thing that 19th-century critics such as Hazlitt see is the play's debt to the classical tradition. Coleridge, too, finds fault with *Volpone*; however, his objections are slightly different than Dibdin's and Hazlitt's, for they grow out of the sentimental desire to see human decency represented. He argues:

This admirable, indeed, but yet more wonderful than admirable, play is from the fertility and vigour of invention, character, language, and sentiment the strongest proof, how impossible it is to keep up any pleasurable interest in a tale, in which there is no goodness of heart in any of the prominent characters. (quoted in Barish, pp. 50–1)

Coleridge then goes on to suggest that Bonario and Celia be made the central figures of the work. This suggestion shows the Romantic need for heroes who crusade against tyranny and injustice. It also demonstrates the inability of those in the 19th century to appreciate Jonson's brand of cynicism. With such attitudes and prejudices it is little wonder that the play fails to receive a single production in the 19th century.

Although the English writer Algernon Charles Swinburne writes a spirited defense of *Volpone* in 1889, it is not until the 20th century that the critical fortunes of Jonson and *Volpone* turn again. No one is more responsible for this change in critical valuation than the poet T.S. Eliot and the scholars/editors C.H. Herford, Percy Simpson and Evelyn Simpson. Eliot's 1919 essay on Ben Jonson begins the process of rescuing the playwright from his own reputation. Claiming that Jonson's writing is as enjoyable as it is scholarly, Eliot persuasively argues:

> [Jonson] has suffered from his great reputation as a critic and theorist, from the effects of his intelligence. We have been taught to think of him as the man, the dictator (confusedly in our minds with his later namesake), as the literary politician impressing his views upon a generation; we are offended by the constant reminder of his scholarship. We forget the comedy in the humours, and the serious artist in the scholar. Jonson has suffered in public opinion, as any one must suffer who is forced to talk about his art. (p. 134)

Referencing *Volpone* and several other plays, Eliot also defends Jonson's method of characterization as well as his verse. By connecting situation, character and language, Eliot successfully shows that Jonson's plays are highly integrated, complex works of art and not simply superficial treatments of characters uttering stultified verse. Concurrent with Eliot's essay (and the 1921 production of *Volpone* by the Phoenix Society) is the work of C.H. Herford and Percy and Evelyn Simpson on their 11-volume Oxford edition of Jonson's complete works. The project, which begins in 1902 and is complete with the publication of the final volume in 1952, is unanimously accepted as the single most important piece of Jonsonian scholarship to date. Through their rigorous editing and comprehensive survey of Jonson's literary accomplishments, Herford and the Simpsons almost singlehandedly revive Jonson in scholarly circles. In short, the Oxford edition makes Jonson once again an author worthy of study (and theatrical production).

By the middle of the 20th century, efforts to rehabilitate the image of the fallen playwright and poet are largely complete. This change in the general perception of Jonson frees scholars to focus more narrowly on individual plays in the latter half of the 20th century. Of the many who come to *Volpone*'s defense during this period, none does so with more ardor than Jonas Barish. Working primarily in the 1950s, 60s and 70s, Barish mounts a series of impassioned arguments on behalf of *Volpone*. Barish's criticism sweeps away many of the false accusations that have been leveled against the play. Specifically, Barish builds on the work of Swinburne and Herford by demonstrating the relationship between the events of the final act and Volpone's personality. More importantly, Barish's 1953 essay 'The Double Plot in *Volpone*' powerfully rebuts earlier claims that the Sir Pol scenes are irrelevant and mere 'excrescencies'. By linking Sir Pol and Lady Would-be to the play's tone and themes, Barish helps make a much-maligned section of *Volpone* appear a vital part of the whole again. In short, Barish's emphasis on the total structure of the play encourages readers to focus on the ways in which all elements of *Volpone* – plot, character, theme, language and theatricality – are interconnected. Barish's approach, like Eliot's approach, is in sharp contrast to earlier critics' fixation on individual incidents, characters or lines of text; and it greatly increases the estimation of *Volpone*'s literary merit in scholarly circles.

By the latter part of the 20th century, Ben Jonson's place in the list of the world's most important writers is firmly established. So too is *Volpone*'s place in the canon of great dramatic works. Throughout the process of rehabilitating and resurrecting both playwright and play, modern scholars have mostly chosen to ignore the shortcomings of Jonson and *Volpone*. When both regained their rightful place in the pantheon of literary excellence, scholars could once again explore the limitations of Jonson's writing without jeopardizing his standing in the literary community. Although her opinion is not universally shared, Anne Barton's 1984 assessment probably best captures the late 20th-century appraisal of Jonson and his plays:

> Certainly it is true that he has fewer readers than he deserves, and that the contemporary theatre (which ought to know better) appears nervously unwilling to trust him. Jonson himself must bear part of the blame for his ossification in the minds of later generations. The severity, exclusiveness and authoritarian nature of many of his critical and moral pronouncements, the classicism and conservatism so strenuously advanced, have all too often managed to block out the other, and artistically equally fertile, if formally less well defined side of his personality and art. (pp. ix–x)

By mentioning Jonson's shortcomings even as she defends him, Barton acknowledges the reasons for his unpopularity without letting those reasons diminish her overall appreciation of Jonson's work. This balanced approach remains a useful lens through which one can view Jonson's oeuvre.

Since Barton, little has been written about the literary merit of *Volpone*. Commenting on the dearth of 21st-century appraisals of *Volpone*'s artistry, Robert Evans writes:

> Ironically, the category of commentary that seems to have received least attention from recent students of *Volpone* is the category that is arguably most important: the category dealing with the play's craftsmanship, or with its features or successes as a work of art.... Recent discussion of *Volpone* as a compelling demonstration of Jonson's talent as a writer and of his skill as a playwright has been relatively rare. Perhaps critics feel that all that can be said on this subject has been said already; perhaps they feel that the artistic merits of the play are so obvious that they need little sustained attention.... Whatever the reasons, it is striking that attention to the artistry and craft of *Volpone* has been the subject of so little extended discussion in recent writing about the play. (p. 71)

Evans is probably right that the current critical silence reflects the fact that a general consensus about the work seems to have been reached; nevertheless, the lack of scholarship on this subject could be a troubling trend if it persists. Critics are not just interpreters of plays; they are also advocates for them, and if no one is speaking on behalf of *Volpone*, then there is a danger that it could once again disappear from the repertory. Scholarship and production do not exist in two separate vacuums, so it is not unreasonable to theorize that there might even be a connection between the shortage of 21st-century productions of *Volpone* and the relative silence from contemporary scholars about the play's artistic virtues. As with the play's recent production history, it is still too early to say whether this current phenomenon merely represents a brief pause after a flurry of activity or if it is the beginning of a much larger trend of scholarly neglect.

Critical interpretation

When considering the critical literature dedicated to *Volpone*, it is also necessary to examine how modern scholars from various schools of literary criticism have interpreted the play. Each school of criticism has its own methodology and concerns; for example, Marxist criticism looks at the relationship between the work and various economic systems while postcolonial criticism looks at how the text depicts colonial oppression and anticolonial resistance. Each approach functions as a lens through which the reader can experience and engage with the work. Critics from nearly every school of criticism have interpreted *Volpone*; however, certain approaches have proved more useful and durable than others. The approaches that are most prevalent in the recent critical discourse surrounding the play are feminist criticism, psychoanalytic literary criticism, New Historicism and performance criticism.

Feminist criticism studies the explicit and implicit attitudes toward women in a given text. Furthermore, it examines how a text's approach to gender challenges and/or reinforces the disenfranchisement of women. Traditionally, feminist critics have not viewed Jonson's work in a positive light. In her book *Renaissance Dramatists*, Kathleen McLuskie succinctly expresses these critics' general opinion of Jonson's writing:

> In his list of women characters, the familiar figures of comic misogyny recur, from the empty-headed court lady, fit only for the attentions of equally foolish men, through the unsexed middle-aged woman, affecting learning or religion, to the empty cipher of the virtuous girl who exists only as a pawn in male games of power or wit or money.... Jonson deals in his comedies primarily with the leisured male world of the street and the

> market-place: in that world women initiate no plots, solve no problems, and the plays offer no insight into specifically female preoccupations. (p. 159)

It is not difficult to see how *Volpone* fits neatly into this understanding of Jonson's work. Celia is the virtuous cipher with no autonomy while Lady Would-be is the middle-aged woman pretending to be educated. All power in the play resides in the hands of men, and the women are important only to the extent that they become involved in the men's game. Helen Ostovich's essay 'Ben Jonson and the Dynamics of Misogyny: A Cultural Collaboration' challenges this view of Jonson's writing. Ostovich does not deny the existence of misogynistic elements in Jonson's plays; however, she does argue that Jonson's middle comedies present a mixed message about the role of women in Jacobean society. In her analysis of *Volpone*, Ostovich identifies two models of womanhood in the play: the chaste and silent bride (Celia) and the domineering and insatiable Amazon (Lady Would-be). These categories, though, are blurred as a result of the male gaze. (Corvino and Volpone perceive Celia as a slut while Sir Pol experiences Lady Would-be as a paragon of virtue.) This fluidity, Ostovich suggests, may have led Jacobean women to conceive of their sexuality in a way other than the virgin-whore dichotomy dictates. Even though Ostovich's position remains a minority position in the scholarly community, it does demonstrate the possibility of more nuanced feminist approaches to *Volpone*.

Although there are many strands of psychoanalytic literary criticism, in its most basic form it looks at literature through the lens of Freudian psychoanalysis. Using terminology and methods developed by Freud and others, psychoanalytic critics explore either the psychology of the author or the psychology of a particular character. Those trying to unearth the mental state of the author will look at his/her work for clues to various neuroses that the writer might suffer from. Those examining the psychology of a fictional character may treat the character as a psychological case study and explain his/her behavior by citing an array of concepts found in Freud or other branches of psychology. Edmund Wilson is the first critic to examine Ben Jonson's work from this perspective. In his essay 'Morose Ben Jonson', Wilson labels Jonson an *anal erotic*, which is a Freudian personality type known for possessing an excessive desire for order and a penchant for hoarding. Wilson points to the precise structure of Jonson's plays as evidence that Jonson has an unhealthy obsession with order. He also cites prefatory materials, such as the Epistle and prologue to *Volpone*, as additional proof of Jonson's need to control and arrange things in a tidy manner. Regarding Jonson's predisposition toward hoarding, Wilson argues that Jonson projects this personality trait onto many of his main characters, including Volpone and Corvino. In Wilson's opinion, both Volpone's steady accumulation of wealth and Corvino's extreme possessiveness of Celia are manifestations of Jonson's own withholding impulse. Ultimately, Wilson's portrait of Jonson and his writing is highly unflattering, but this makes sense given that his stated objective is to use Freud's theories to explain Jonson's unpopularity. For a more positive view of Jonson's life and works, one can turn to David Riggs' psychological biography *Ben Jonson: A Life*. In describing his methodology, Riggs says the following:

> I analyze Jonson's behavior from two complementary points of view. When he is acting like a professional artist making practical choices, I adopt the outlook of the social historian. ... When Jonson's behavior resists that kind of explanation, I seek out a psychological one. These parts of my narrative are frankly speculative and treat the ramifications of his childhood experience, the enactment of persistent neurotic impulses, and the therapeutic functions of his writing. (p. 2)

Riggs employs this two-pronged approach in his analysis of *Volpone*. He observes that the play is both a professional and personal turning point for Jonson. Written just after Jonson's reconciliation with his estranged wife and on the heels of his final arrest, *Volpone* is an indicator that Jonson has reformed his ways. According to Riggs, *Volpone* demonstrates Jonson's maturity and his newfound ability to sublimate negative behaviors, such as lust and aggression, into creative output. For Riggs, Volpone is an extension of Jonson's own worst traits. The playwright identifies with his antihero 'because his own instinctual drives [have] taken him down the very path that leads Volpone to ruin', and as a result of having made that journey, Jonson can now use his art to warn theatergoers about the dangers of following such a self-destructive path (p. 139). In his essay 'Jonsonian Comedy and the Discovery of the Social Self', Lawrence Danson adopts a different approach. He focuses on the psychology of Jonson's characters and not on the psychology of Jonson. In addition, he looks at *Volpone* less through the lens of Freudian psychology and more through the lens of social psychology. Danson contends that the characters in *Volpone* have no authentic psychological self to discover and that their identities are determined almost entirely by a series of unstable social interactions and situations. For Jonson's characters a shift in context inexorably alters their identities. This is in marked contrast to Shakespeare's comic characters who eventually discover their true selves as their social and familial relationships stabilize in the comedy's final act. By noting that Jonson's characters experience no such discovery, Danson moves the psychoanalytic study of *Volpone* away from an examination of personality and toward an examination of social interactions. At the moment it is unclear whether Danson's approach is an aberration or the beginning of a larger shift.

New Historicists connect a work of literature to the time period in which it is written. They focus on historical events as well as political, cultural and literary movements that may have influenced either the writing or interpretation of the work. Numerous critics have looked at *Volpone* from this vantage point. Three of the most interesting studies come from Stephen Greenblatt, Robert C. Evans and Richard Dutton. Greenblatt's essay 'The False Ending in *Volpone*' argues that Volpone's seeming triumph at the end of Act IV is a structural device borrowed from Christopher Marlowe's *Jew of Malta*, for in both plays the titular character experiences a near defeat followed by a miraculous resurrection and a final catastrophe. In addition, Greenblatt connects Volpone's sense of identity to new Renaissance ideas about the self and the possibility of self-consciousness. Evans chooses to focus on the relationship between the character of Volpone and Thomas Sutton, the wealthiest common citizen in Jacobean England. Evans' monograph *Jonson and the Contexts of His Time* includes a chapter entitled 'Thomas Sutton: Jonson's Volpone?' in which Evans investigates the frequent 17th-century claim that the character of Volpone is modeled after Sutton. Although most scholars have dismissed the claim as baseless, Evans mounts a persuasive case that there is a connection between Volpone and Sutton. He notes Sutton's reclusive nature, lack of close relations and frequent revising of his will as possible parallels between the two men. After reading Evans' analysis, it is difficult to reject the possibility that *Volpone* is either a satire of Sutton or that it at least would have been perceived as such by many in Jacobean England. In his book *Jonson, Volpone and the Gunpowder Plot*, Dutton also sees the makings of personal satire in *Volpone*; however, he identifies a different target: Robert Cecil, the most powerful political figure in England behind King James I and the man behind the discovery of the Gunpowder Plot of 1605. Disliked and feared by most English Catholics, Cecil is a logical target for a convert such as Jonson. Similar to Evans, Dutton sees Jonson's fierce denial of personal satire in the Epistle as evidence that such satire either exists or is being perceived by theatergoers and readers. He also notes Jonson's use of the beast fable, a form that had previously been used to satirize Cecil. In addition, Dutton maintains that Sir Pol's frequent use of the word 'plot' and the play's preoccupation with conspiracies are both part of Jonson's attempt to craft an oblique response to the events surrounding the Gunpowder Plot. Unlike Evans, Dutton does not see Jonson's target embodied in a specific character; instead, he sees the entire play as a satirical meditation on Cecil, power and conspiracies. While an intriguing read, Dutton's monograph ultimately suffers from his own admission that he lacks a 'smoking gun which convicts Jonson of writing an anti-Cecil play in *Volpone*' (p. 133). The absence of such proof reduces his argument to little more than interesting inference.

Performance criticism refers to academic discourse that explores how a play is realized (i.e., stage histories) or could be realized in production. Because the vast majority of this book is a form of performance criticism, little attention will be given to other examples of performance criticism here; however, those looking for additional works of performance criticism should consult Richard Allen Cave's *Ben Jonson*. Cave focuses extensively on the metatheatricality of *Volpone*, noting that Jonson utilizes 'ideas of acting, playwriting, [and] improvisation in a series of conceits to illuminate the nature of greed' (p. 55). He then goes on to explore how this metatheatricality can be harnessed to give *Volpone* a 'powerful and disturbing immediacy' in performance (p. 55). Cave, an opponent of cutting the text for performance, also examines the problems associated with editing *Volpone* and provides an informed, albeit biased, account of several modern productions. Although Cave is probably too dogmatic in his approach to *Volpone*, his strong opinions prompt the reader to contemplate the best ways of staging Jonson's extraordinary comedy about vice, greed and performance.

The diversity of the critical responses to *Volpone* is a testament to its brilliance and complexity. All great works of art should yield a myriad of interpretations, and *Volpone* certainly does this. None of the critics cited in this chapter will have the final word on the meaning of *Volpone*, nor should they. They are merely participants in a centuries-old conversation about a challenging play that will continue to inspire debate and contemplation for many years to come.

Further Reading

The volume of critical material devoted to Jonson's life and work can be overwhelming. The books and scholarly articles on *Volpone* alone could fill a bookcase. This list barely scratches the surface of all the available critical literature; nevertheless, the books and articles below represent a good starting point for anyone looking to delve deeper into this masterful play. I would especially recommend the scholarship of R.B. Parker (sometimes cited as Brian Parker), Richard Dutton and Jonas Barish.

1 The text and early performances

Editions

Revels Plays: ed. Brian Parker (Manchester: Manchester University Press, 1999). The most rigorously edited edition with comprehensive footnotes, a superb introduction and appendices that deal with the source material.

London Medieval and Renaissance Series: ed. John Creaser (London: Hodder & Stoughton, 1978). A highly respected edition with an introduction that offers insight into the motivation and psychology of the play's central characters.

Ben Jonson, gen. eds C.H. Herford, Percy Simpson and Evelyn Simpson, 11 vols (Oxford: Clarendon Press, 1925–52). The definitive version of Jonson's works and the source for almost all subsequent scholarship; a critical introduction can be found in volume II, the full text in volume V and a production history in volume IX.

Ben Jonson and publication

Jonas Barish, 'Jonson and the Loathèd Stage', in William Blissett, Julian Patrick and R.W. Van Fossen (eds), *A Celebration of Ben Jonson* (Toronto:

University of Toronto Press, 1973), pp. 27–53. A provocative piece that explores Jonson's ambivalence toward the stage as well as his role in preparing texts for print.

Richard Dutton, 'The Lone Wolf: Jonson's Epistle to *Volpone*', in Julie Sanders, Kate Chedgzoy and Susan Wiseman (eds), *Refashioning Ben Jonson: Gender, Politics, and the Jonsonian Canon* (Basingstoke: Macmillan, 1998), pp. 114–33. An essay that connects the content and tone of the Epistle to Jonson's legal troubles.

Early productions

Robert Gale Noyes, *Ben Jonson on the English Stage: 1660–1776* (Cambridge: Harvard University Press, 1935). A comprehensive study of all early productions of Jonson's work, including those before 1660.

2 Cultural contexts and sources

Economic context

L.C. Knights, *Drama and Society in the Age of Jonson* (New York: W.W. Norton & Company, 1937). Written from a Marxist perspective, a landmark study of the relationship between the Elizabethan-Jacobean economy and the dramatic works of the epoch.

Sean McEvoy, *Ben Jonson, Renaissance Dramatist* (Edinburgh: Edinburgh University Press, 2008). A survey of Jonson's dramatic output with relevant historical and literary contexts included.

Don E. Wayne, 'Drama and Society in the Age of Jonson: An Alternate View', in Richard Dutton (ed.), *Longman Critical Readers: Ben Jonson* (Harlow: Pearson Education, 2000), pp. 26–49. A rethinking of Knights' claim that Jonson is a traditionalist critiquing the nascent capitalist economy of Jacobean England.

Literary context

Brian Gibbons, *Jacobean City Comedy: A Study of Satiric Plays by Jonson, Marston and Middleton* (Cambridge: Harvard University Press, 1968). An overview of the genre from its beginnings in 1597 to its apotheosis in 1616.

Coburn Gum, *The Aristophanic Comedies of Ben Jonson* (The Hague: Mouton & Company, 1969). A comparison of Aristophanes' and Jonson's writing that asserts Jonson's plays owe much of their structure, method of characterization and style to Aristophanes.

Primary sources

Aesop, *The Complete Fables*, trans. by Olivia and Robert Temple (London: Penguin, 1998), pp. 26–8, 122, 176 and 257. A source of animal lore in *Volpone*.

The History of Reynard the Fox, translated and printed by William Caxton in 1481, ed. by Donald B. Sands (Cambridge: Harvard University Press, 1960). The most important source of animal lore in *Volpone*.

Horace, *Satires, Epistles and Ars Poetica*, trans. by H. Rushton Fairclough (Cambridge: Harvard University Press, 1926), pp. 196–207 and 442–89. A source for the legacy-hunting narrative and a primary influence on Jonson's literary philosophy.

Lucian, *Lucian*, trans. by M.D. Macleod, 8 vols (Cambridge: Harvard University Press, 1961), VII, pp. 78–101. A source for the legacy-hunting narrative.

Petronius, *The Satyricon*, trans. by William Arrowsmith (Ann Arbor: University of Michigan Press, 1959), pp. 132–5, 151–2 and 177–8. A source for the legacy-hunting narrative.

Analysis of source material

R.B. Parker, '*Volpone* and *Reynard the Fox*', *Renaissance Drama*, 7 (1976), pp. 3–42. An overview of the relationship between the two works.

4 Key productions and performances

General studies

Richard Cave, 'Designing for Jonson's Plays', in Richard Cave, Elizabeth Schafer and Brian Woolland (eds), *Ben Jonson and Theatre: Performance, Practice and Theory* (London: Routledge, 1999), pp. 43–55. A scholarly analysis of the design problems posed by Jonson's plays and an exploration of the solutions devised by various modern productions.

Ejner J. Jensen, *Ben Jonson's Comedies on the Modern Stage* (Ann Arbor: University of Michigan Press, 1985). A work that surveys professional productions of Jonson's comedies between 1921 and 1972.

R.B. Parker, '*Volpone* in Performance: 1921–1972', *Renaissance Drama*, 9 (1978), pp. 147–73. An opinionated production history that explores the benefits and drawbacks of the approaches taken by various directors, actors and designers during this period.

Rebecca Yearling, '*Volpone* on the Stage', in Matthew Steggle (ed.), *Volpone: A Critical Guide* (London: Continuum, 2011), pp. 31–54. A detached production history that reconstructs most major productions through the early 21st century; also a great source of information on adaptations of *Volpone* for the stage and other media.

Specific productions

Michael Billington, 'Vivid *Volpone*', *Guardian*, 29 July 1995. A very positive review of Matthew Warchus' 1995 production of *Volpone* at the National Theatre.

Michael Billington, '*Volpone*', *Guardian*, 27 April 1977. A mixed review of Peter Hall's 1977 production of *Volpone* at the National Theatre.

Jacquelyn Bessell, 'The Actors' Renaissance Season at the Blackfriars Playhouse', in Pascale Aebischer and Kathryn Prince (eds), *Performing Early Modern Drama Today* (Cambridge: Cambridge University Press, 2012), pp. 85–103. A survey of the production and rehearsal practices used during the Actors' Renaissance Season at the American Shakespeare Center.

Nick Curtis, 'Where There's a Will, There's a Way to Inherit', *Evening Standard*, 28 July 1995. A very positive review of Matthew Warchus' 1995 production of *Volpone* at the National Theatre.

T.S. Eliot, 'London Letter: May 1921', in Lawrence Rainey (ed.), *Modernism: An Anthology* (Malden: Blackwell, 2005), pp. 158–9. Reprinted from its original publication in *The Dial*, a firsthand account of the Phoenix Society's historic 1921 revival of *Volpone*.

'Ewan Marshall', in Gabriella Giannachi and Mary Luckhurst (eds), *On Directing: Interviews with Directors* (London: Faber and Faber, 1999), pp. 60-6. An interview with Ewan Marshall, who directed Graeae Theatre Company's production of *Flesh Fly*.

Greg Hersov, personal communication, 26 February 2014. An interview with the director of the Royal Exchange Theatre's 2004 production.

R.B. Parker, 'Wolfit's Fox: An Interpretation of *Volpone*', *University of Toronto Quarterly*, 45 (1976), pp. 200–20. A scholarly reconstruction of the many stagings between 1938 and 1953 that feature Wolfit as Volpone.

'Production Notebook: Red Bull Theater's *Volpone*', *American Theatre Magazine*, 30.2 (2013), pp. 34–5. A short collection of quotations from the director, costume designer and wig designer of Red Bull's 2012 production.

5 The play on screen

Films

The Honey Pot, dir. by Joseph Mankiewicz (MGM, 2010) [on DVD].
Il Volpone, dir. by Maurizio Ponzi (Cecchi Gori Home Video, 2006) [on DVD].

Volpone, dir. by Elizabeth Freestone (Stage on Screen, 2010) [on DVD].
Volpone, dir. by Frédéric Auburtin (Koba Films Video, 2008) [on DVD].
Volpone, dir. by Maurice Tourneur (René Chateau Video, 2006) [on DVD].

Secondary sources

Pascale Aebischer, 'Early Modern Drama on Screen', in Pascale Aebischer and Kathryn Prince (eds), *Performing Early Modern Drama Today* (Cambridge: Cambridge University Press, 2012), pp. 142–61. Focusing primarily on *Volpone* and *The Changeling*, a study of early modern plays by writers other than Shakespeare that have been adapted for the screen.

Sarah Hatchuel and Nathalie Vienne-Guerrin, 'Nationalizing *Volpone* in French Cinema and Television: Mediating Jonson through Molière, Shakespeare and Popular Screen Comedy', *Shakespeare Bulletin*, 29.4 (2011), pp. 509–23. An exploration of the debt that French cinematic adaptations of *Volpone* owe to Shakespeare's *Merchant of Venice*, French comic traditions and French culture.

James M. Welsh, 'Shades of Ben Jonson and Stefan Zweig: *Volpone* on Film', *South Atlantic Bulletin*, 39.4 (1974), pp. 43–50. A study of the differences and similarities between Jonson's original, Zweig's adaptation and Tourneur's film.

Stefan Zweig, *Volpone: A Loveless Comedy in 3 Acts*, trans. by Ruth Langner (New York: Viking Press, 1928). A stage adaptation that inspired Tourneur's film.

6 Critical assessments

Critical valuation

Jonas Barish (ed.), *Jonson: Volpone, A Casebook* (London: Macmillan, 1972). A collection of critical materials, including excerpts from most major commentaries written between 1662 and 1919.

Anne Barton, *Ben Jonson, Dramatist* (Cambridge: Cambridge University Press, 1984). A study of Jonson's entire dramatic corpus with a focus on the contributions and quality of each individual play.

D.H. Craig (ed.), *Ben Jonson: The Critical Heritage 1599–1798* (London: Routledge, 1990). A compilation of all critical assessments of Jonson's work between 1599 and 1798.

T.S. Eliot, 'Ben Jonson', in *Selected Essays* (New York: Harcourt, Brace & World, 1969), pp. 127–39. Reprinted following its initial publication in 1919, an essential piece of criticism that lays the groundwork for a reconsideration of Jonson in the 20th century.

Robert C. Evans, 'The State of the Art', in Matthew Steggle (ed.), *Volpone: A Critical Guide* (London: Continuum, 2011), pp. 55–82. A comprehensive study of critical literature devoted to *Volpone* between 2001 and 2010.

Critical interpretation

Richard Allen Cave, *Ben Jonson* (New York: Saint Martin's Press, 1991). A survey of Jonson's dramatic works with an emphasis on the plays in performance.

Lawrence Danson, 'Jonsonian Comedy and the Discovery of the Social Self', *Publications of the Modern Language Association*, 99.2 (1984), pp. 179–93. A psychoanalytic reading that uses the principles of social psychology to analyze Jonson's method of characterization in *Cynthia's Revels, Every Man Out of His Humour* and *Volpone*.

Richard Dutton, *Ben Jonson, Volpone and the Gunpowder Plot* (Cambridge: Cambridge University Press, 2008). A New Historicist reading of *Volpone* that sees the play as an anti-Cecil satire informed by Catholic anxiety over the government's response to the Gunpowder Plot of 1605.

Robert C. Evans, *Jonson and the Contexts of His Time* (Lewisburg: Bucknell University Press, 1994). A New Historicist study that includes a chapter on the relationship between the character of Volpone and Thomas Sutton, Jacobean England's wealthiest common citizen.

Stephen Greenblatt, 'The False Ending in *Volpone*', *Journal of English and Germanic Philology*, 75 (1976), pp. 90–104. A New Historicist reading that focuses on the fourth and fifth acts of *Volpone*.

Kathleen McLuskie, *Renaissance Dramatists* (Atlantic Highlands: Humanities Press International, 1989). A feminist survey of English Renaissance drama that includes a chapter devoted to Ben Jonson.

Helen Ostovich, 'Ben Jonson and the Dynamics of Misogyny: A Cultural Collaboration', *Elizabethan Theatre*, XV (2002), pp. 89–109. A feminist reading that explores the ways in which Jonson's middle comedies reinforce and challenge the misogynistic attitudes of Jacobean England.

David Riggs, *Ben Jonson: A Life* (Cambridge: Harvard University Press, 1989). A biography that uses both history and Freudian psychology to give readers a picture of Jonson's life and personality.

Edmund Wilson, 'Morose Ben Jonson', in *The Triple Thinkers: Twelve Essays on Literary Subjects* (New York: Oxford University Press, 1948), pp. 213–32. An unflattering Freudian reading of Jonson that paints him as an *anal erotic* whose writing suffers from an unhealthy obsession with order.

Index

Aesop
 Fables, 14, 17
Alexander, Bill, 92
Almeida Theatre, 92–3
American Shakespeare Center, 97–9
Aristophanes, 10–12
Auburtin, Frédéric
 Volpone (2003), 109–10

Barish, Jonas, 1, 32, 119
Baur, Harry, 106
Beale, Simon Russell, 93–4
Billington, Michael, 91, 94
Burbage, Richard, 4

Carroll, Pat, 96
Cave, Richard Allen, 93, 125
Cavendish, Margaret, 115
Cecil, Robert, 125
City Comedy, 13–14
Coleridge, Samuel Taylor, 117–18

Depardieu, Gérard, 109
Dryden, John, 114–15
Dutton, Richard, 124–5

Eliot, T.S., 85–6, 118
Evans, Robert C., 120, 124–5

feminist criticism, 121–2
Folio (1616), 1–2, 4
Freestone, Elizabeth
 Volpone (2010), 102–3

Gambon, Michael, 93–4
Globe Theatre, 5
Graeae Theatre Company, 94–5
Greenblatt, Stephen, 124
Griffiths, Richard, 92
Gunpowder Plot, 125
Guthrie, Tyrone, 90

Hall, Peter, 91
Harrison, Rex, 106
Hazlitt, William, 117
Herford, C.H., 118–19
History of Reynard the Fox, The, 14, 17–18
Horace
 Ars Poetica, 10–11
 Satires, 14–15
Hytner, Nicholas, 92–3

James I, 3, 23, 125
Jonson, Ben
 Alchemist, The, 13–14
 Bartholomew Fair, 13, 64
 Eastward Ho, 3, 5
 Epicene, 5, 13
 Sejanus, 5

Kahn, Michael, 95–6
Knights, L.C., 8

Littlewood, Joan, 84, 89–90
Lucian
 Dialogues of the Dead, 14, 16

Mankiewicz, Joseph
  Honey Pot, The, 106–7, 110
Marlowe, Christopher
  Jew of Malta, The, 124

National Theatre, 90–1, 93–4
Neoclassicism, 4, 6, 20, 111–15
New Historicism, 124–5

Parker, R.B., 17–18, 46, 88, 90, 102
Pepys, Samuel, 5
performance criticism, 125
Petronius
  Satyricon, The, 15–16
Phoenix Society, 6, 85–6
Plautus, 10–12, 117
Ponzi, Maurizio
  Il Volpone, 108
psychoanalytic criticism, 122–4

Quarto (1607), 1–2, 11, 111–12

Red Bull Theater, 99–101
Robertson, Cliff, 106

Romains, Jules, 104–5
romantic comedy, 13–14
Romanticism, 6, 116–18
Royal Exchange Theatre, 97–8
Royal Shakespeare Company, 92, 96

Scofield, Paul, 91
Shaban, Nabil, 95
Shakespeare Theatre Company, 95–6
Shakespeare, William, 1, 40–1, 106, 117, 124
Simpson, Percy, 118–19
Smith, Maggie, 106
Sutton, Thomas, 12, 124–5

Tourneur, Maurice
  Volpone (1941), 104–6

Warchus, Matthew, 93–4
Wilson, Edmund, 122–3
Wolfit, Donald, 86–8, 102

Zweig, Stefan, 104–6